Vanessa-Ann's

Holidays In Cross-Stitch

1993

The Vanessa-Ann Collection Staff

Owners: Jo Packham and Terrece Beesley

Sandra Durbin Chapman

Kristi Glissmeyer

Susan Jorgensen

Margaret Shields Marti

Barbara Milburn

Lisa Miles

Pamela Randall

Jennifer Roberts

Florence Stacey

Nancy Whitley

Gloria Zirkel

Designers

Marina Anderson

Terrece Beesley

Trice Boerens

Dale Bryner

Susan Cottrell

Doug Simmons

Julie Truman Steinkopf

Vanessa-Ann's
Holidays In Cross-Stitch
1993

This volume is a thank-you especially for Laurie—for her friendship, for her expertise, and for her thoughtful care in the preparation of many of our books.
                    —from her friends at Vanessa-Ann

©1992 by Oxmoor House, Inc.
Book Division of Southern Progress Corporation
P.O. Box 2463, Birmingham, Alabama 35201

All designs that appear in this book are the property of Chapelle Designers, Ltd., Ogden, Utah.
Library of Congress Catalog Number: 86-62285
ISBN: 0-8487-1086-X
ISSN: 0890-8230
Manufactured in the United States of America
First Printing 1992

Editor-in-Chief: Nancy Janice Fitzpatrick
Senior Crafts Editor: Susan Ramey Wright
Senior Editor, Editorial Services: Olivia Wells
Director of Manufacturing: Jerry Higdon
Art Director: James Boone

Holidays In Cross-Stitch 1993

Editor: Laurie Pate Sewell
Editorial Assistant: Patricia Weaver
Copy Chief: Mary Jean Haddin
Copy Editor: Susan Smith Cheatham
Assistant Copy Editor: L. Amanda Owens
Production Manager: Rick Litton
Associate Production Manager: Theresa L. Beste
Production Assistant: Pam Beasley Bullock
Designer: Diana Smith Morrison
Computer Artist: Karen Tindall Tillery
Artist: Eleanor Cameron
Photographer: Ryne Hazen
Framer: Artist Touch

The Vanessa-Ann Collection thanks the following people for their continued support and trust in allowing us to photograph at their locations: Mary Gaskill at Trends and Traditions, Ogden, Utah; Becky Tuttle in Orem, Utah; Anita Louise's Bearlace Cottage in Park City, Utah; and Jo Packham in Ogden, Utah.

1993

Contents

Introduction 6

JANUARY 1 ❧ New Year's Day
Confetti Runner 9

JANUARY 6 ❧ Carl Sandburg's Birthday
Tears of Joy............................13

FEBRUARY 14 ❧ Valentine's Day
Everlasting Love 16
Cushioned with Love 19

FEBRUARY 15 ❧ Presidents' Day
Americana 23

MARCH 1 ❧ National Pig Day
For the Love of Pigs 28

MARCH 5–7 ❧ Mountain Memories Weekend
The Hunt 32

APRIL 6–13 ❧ Passover
Star of David Cloth................36

APRIL 11 ❧ Easter
Bunny Buddies.......................40

APRIL 18–24 ❧ National Wildlife Week
Grizzly...................................51

APRIL 22 ❧ Earth Day Anniversary
Earth Awareness....................54

MAY ❧ National Home Decorating Month
Miniature Cushions 58

MAY 7–9 ❧ Wildflower Weekend
Wildflowers in Bloom.............62

MAY 9 ❧ Mother's Day
Hearts & Flowers Tea Towels 67

JUNE ❧ National Adopt-a-Cat Month
The "Purrfect" Wall Hanging 72

JUNE 18–20 ❧ Wizard of Oz Convention
Pajama Bag 77

JUNE 27 ❧ Singing on the Mountain
Sweet Sounds of Summer......83

JULY 11 ❧ Old Crafts Day
Old-fashioned Sewing Box 86

AUGUST 12 ❧ Baby Parade
Storybook Animals.................90

SEPTEMBER 6 ❧ Jane Addams' Birthday
Sachet Doll 93

SEPTEMBER 26 ❧ National Good Neighbor Day
Welcome, Neighbor 98

OCTOBER ❧ Wine Festival Month
Time for Wine......................103

OCTOBER 3–9 ❧ National Newspaper Week
Newsletters 107

OCTOBER 10–16 ❧ National Job Skills Week
When I Grow Up 110

NOVEMBER 17 ❧ National Young Reader's Day
The Magic of a Book 121

NOVEMBER 25 ❧ Thanksgiving
Give Thanks 125

DECEMBER 24 ❧ Christmas Eve
Toyland Stocking..................128

DECEMBER 25 ❧ Christmas Day
Santa Trio 134
Julnisse................................139

General Instructions.......142
Suppliers 144
Jacket Motif (Border).....144

Introduction

Celebrate a glorious new year with an abundance of innovative cross-stitch projects from The Vanessa-Ann Collection. Everyone loves a holiday, and in *Holidays In Cross-Stitch 1993*, we have combined traditional celebrations with some not-so-familiar festivities to bring you something fun and unique to stitch throughout the year. We at Vanessa-Ann wish you many hours of stitching enjoyment and hope that our designs will make every day a holiday.

1993

JANUARY
S	M	T	W	T	F	S
					(1)	2
3	4	5	(6)	7	8	9
10	11	12	13	14	15	16
17	18	19	20	21	22	23
24	25	26	27	28	29	30
31						

FEBRUARY
S	M	T	W	T	F	S
	1	2	3	4	5	6
7	8	9	10	11	12	13
(14)	(15)	16	17	18	19	20
21	22	23	24	25	26	27
28						

MARCH
S	M	T	W	T	F	S
	(1)	2	3	4	(5)	6
7	8	9	10	11	12	13
14	15	16	17	18	19	20
21	22	23	24	25	26	27
28	29	30	31			

APRIL
S	M	T	W	T	F	S
				1	2	3
4	5	(6)	7	8	9	10
(11)	12	13	14	(15)	16	17
(18)	19	20	21	(22)	23	24
25	26	27	28	29	30	

MAY
S	M	T	W	T	F	S
						(1)
2	3	4	5	6	(7)	8
(9)	10	11	12	13	14	15
16	17	18	19	20	21	22
23	24	25	26	27	28	29
30	31					

JUNE
S	M	T	W	T	F	S
	(1)	2	3	4	5	
6	7	8	9	10	11	12
13	14	15	16	17	(18)	19
20	21	22	23	24	25	26
(27)	28	29	30			

JULY
S	M	T	W	T	F	S
				1	2	3
4	5	6	7	8	9	10
(11)	12	13	14	15	16	17
18	19	20	21	22	23	24
25	26	27	28	29	30	31

AUGUST
S	M	T	W	T	F	S
1	2	3	4	5	6	7
8	9	10	11	(12)	13	14
15	16	17	18	19	20	21
22	23	24	25	26	27	28
29	30	31				

SEPTEMBER
S	M	T	W	T	F	S
			1	2	3	4
5	(6)	7	8	9	10	11
12	13	14	15	16	17	18
19	20	21	22	23	24	25
(26)	27	28	29	30		

OCTOBER
S	M	T	W	T	F	S
					(1)	2
(3)	4	5	6	7	8	9
(10)	11	12	13	14	15	16
17	18	19	20	21	22	23
24	25	26	27	28	29	30
31						

NOVEMBER
S	M	T	W	T	F	S
	1	2	3	4	5	6
7	8	9	10	11	12	13
14	15	16	(17)	18	19	20
21	22	23	24	(25)	26	27
28	29	30				

DECEMBER
S	M	T	W	T	F	S
			1	2	3	4
5	6	7	8	9	10	11
12	13	14	15	16	17	18
19	20	21	22	23	(24)	(25)
26	27	28	29	30	31	

New Year's Day

*These tiny, bright motifs resemble remnants
of confetti from the night before—until you take a
closer look! Collect novelty buttons, beads, and bells
to add even more charm to the edges of
your own needlework creation.*

Confetti Runner

SAMPLE

Stitched on Vanessa-Ann Damask 28 over 1 thread, the finished design size is 5⅛" x 5⅛" for each block. Stitch as many blocks as desired. The fabric was cut 58" x 21½". See Suppliers for material.

FABRICS	DESIGN SIZES
Aida 11	13⅛" x 13"
Aida 14	10⅜" x 10¼"
Aida 18	8⅛" x 8"
Hardanger 22	6⅝" x 6½"

MATERIALS

Completed cross-stitch on Vanessa-Ann Damask 28; matching thread

4½ yards (1½"-wide) cream lace

150 small decorative buttons, pebble beads, and bells

DIRECTIONS

1. To hem runner, turn raw edges under ⅛" twice to back. Slipstitch hem in place.

2. Slipstitch straight edge of lace to right side of hemmed edge of runner, pleating lace at each corner to fit.

3. Sew buttons, beads, and bells to edges of runner as desired (see photo).

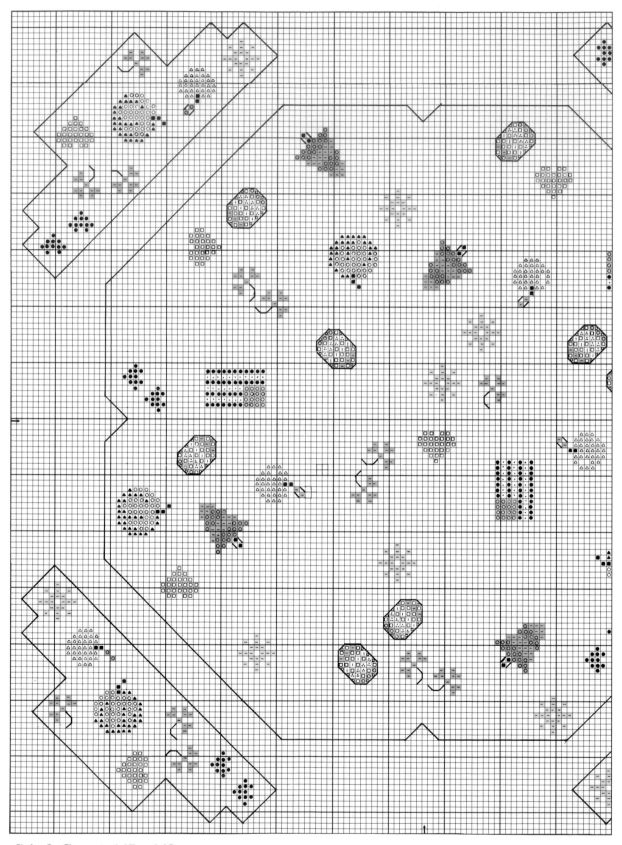

Stitch Count: 145 x 143

10

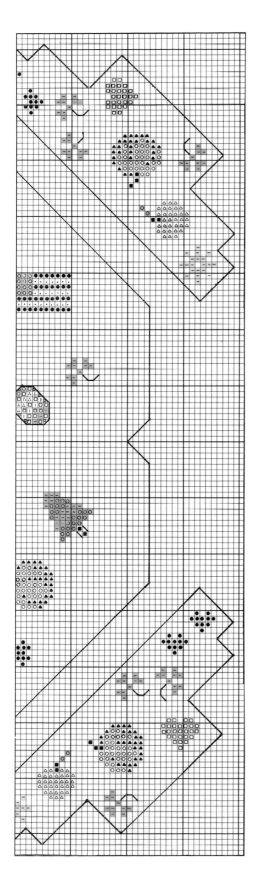

Anchor   **DMC (used for sample)**

Step 1: Cross-stitch (1 strand)

Anchor	Symbol	DMC	Name
1	·		White
301	ı	744	Yellow-pale
316	○	971	Pumpkin
324	▲	721	Orange Spice-med.
26	□ / ◿	894	Carnation-vy. lt.
46	△	666	Christmas Red-bright
13	●	349	Coral-dk.
95	∴	554	Violet-lt.
130	−	794	Cornflower Blue-lt.
121	◐	793	Cornflower Blue-med.
210	−	562	Jade-med.
246	◯	319	Pistachio Green-vy. dk.
379	■	840	Beige Brown-med.

Step 2: Backstitch (1 strand)

Anchor	DMC	Name
26	894	Carnation-vy. lt. (eggs)
13	349	Coral-dk. (flags)
210	562	Jade-med. (four-leaf clover stems)
246	319	Pistachio Green-vy. dk. (apple leaves)
379	840	Beige Brown-med. (all else)

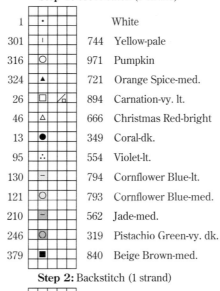
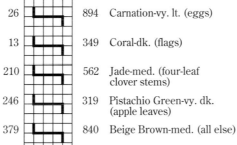

JANUARY 6
Carl Sandburg's Birthday

*One way to make a beautiful thing last
forever is to re-create it in elegant cross-stitch. Carl
Sandburg's touching words are immortalized through
their gentle beauty. His sincere thoughts warm the
heart and soul on many a cold and dreary winter
day, as will this delicate design.*

Stitch Count: 106 x 122

Tears of Joy

SAMPLE
Stitched on white Belfast Linen 32 over 2 threads, the finished design size is 6⅝" x 7⅝". The fabric was cut 13" x 14".

FABRICS	DESIGN SIZES
Aida 11	9⅝" x 11⅛"
Aida 14	7⅝" x 8¾"
Aida 18	5⅞" x 6¾"
Hardanger 22	4⅞" x 5½"

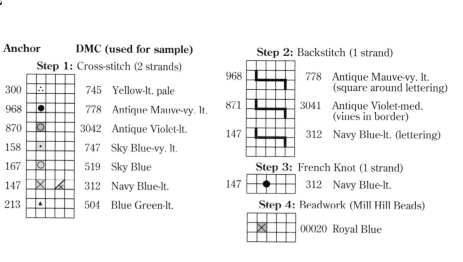

Anchor		DMC (used for sample)
Step 1: Cross-stitch (2 strands)		
300	∴	745 Yellow-lt. pale
968	●	778 Antique Mauve-vy. lt.
870	⊙	3042 Antique Violet-lt.
158	·	747 Sky Blue-vy. lt.
167	◎	519 Sky Blue
147	✕ ╱	312 Navy Blue-lt.
213	▲	504 Blue Green-lt.

Step 2: Backstitch (1 strand)		
968		778 Antique Mauve-vy. lt. (square around lettering)
871		3041 Antique Violet-med. (vines in border)
147		312 Navy Blue-lt. (lettering)

Step 3: French Knot (1 strand)		
147	●	312 Navy Blue-lt.

Step 4: Beadwork (Mill Hill Beads)		
	✕	00020 Royal Blue

FEBRUARY 14
Valentine's Day

*On this special day
set aside for romance,
recapture the magic that
you shared on your
wedding day and enjoy it
for a lifetime with this
delicately stitched
marriage certificate. The
cascading flowers and
soft, subtle shades
will make this piece a
wonderful heirloom.
The sponge-painted child's
chair with stenciled
hearts and flowers and
sweet sentiment will also
become a cherished
treasure to be shared with
children of generations
yet to come.*

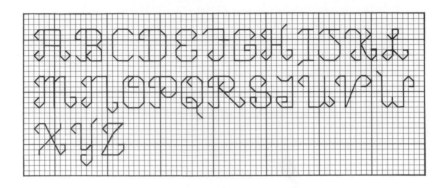

Everlasting Love

SAMPLE
Stitched on cream Belfast Linen 32 over 2 threads, finished design size is 9¾" x 13⅞". Fabric was cut 16" x 20".

FABRICS	DESIGN SIZES
Aida 11	14⅛" x 20¼"
Aida 14	11⅛" x 15⅞"
Aida 18	8⅝" x 12⅜"
Hardanger 22	7" x 10⅛"

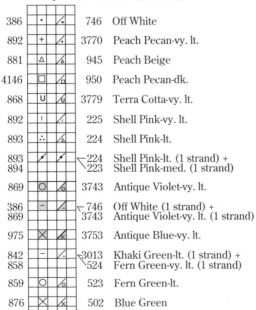

Anchor		DMC (used for sample)	
		Step 1: Cross-stitch (2 strands)	
386		746	Off White
892		3770	Peach Pecan-vy. lt.
881		945	Peach Beige
4146		950	Peach Pecan-dk.
868		3779	Terra Cotta-vy. lt.
892		225	Shell Pink-vy. lt.
893		224	Shell Pink-lt.
893 894		224 223	Shell Pink-lt. (1 strand) + Shell Pink-med. (1 strand)
869		3743	Antique Violet-vy. lt.
386 869		746 3743	Off White (1 strand) + Antique Violet-vy. lt. (1 strand)
975		3753	Antique Blue-vy. lt.
842 858		3013 524	Khaki Green-lt. (1 strand) + Fern Green-vy. lt. (1 strand)
859		523	Fern Green-lt.
876		502	Blue Green

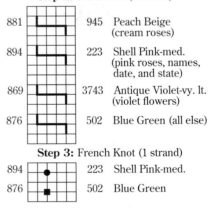

Anchor		DMC (used for sample)	
		Step 2: Backstitch (1 strand)	
881		945	Peach Beige (cream roses)
894		223	Shell Pink-med. (pink roses, names, date, and state)
869		3743	Antique Violet-vy. lt. (violet flowers)
876		502	Blue Green (all else)
		Step 3: French Knot (1 strand)	
894		223	Shell Pink-med.
876		502	Blue Green

On the twenty-sixth of July

in the year of our Lord

nineteen hundred and ninety-one

were united in the holy bond

of matrimony

Witnesses Sara V. Buehler

Justin S. Buehler

Stitch Count: 155 x 223

Cushioned
with Love

SAMPLE
Stitched on ash rose Aida 14 over 1 thread, the finished design size is 5" x 6¼". The fabric was cut 11" x 13".

FABRICS	DESIGN SIZES
Aida 11	6⅜" x 8"
Aida 18	3⅞" x 4⅞"
Hardanger 22	3⅛" x 4"

MATERIALS
Completed cross-stitch on ash rose Aida 14
1 (15" x 15") piece of medium-loft batting
Child's chair
Acrylic paints: light pink, dark pink, yellow, green, blue, cream
Paintbrushes (1 large, 1 small)
Sponge
Stencil brush
Tracing paper
Manila folder
Light green colored pencil
Fine sandpaper
30 brass upholstery tacks

DIRECTIONS

1. With design centered, trim Aida to 8¼" x 9½". Cut 1 (6½" x 7½") batting piece. Cut a second piece of batting ½" smaller on all edges. Set aside.

2. Paint chair with a base coat of light pink; let dry. To sponge-paint chair, apply a small amount of 1 color to dry sponge and dab randomly on wood; let dry. Repeat as desired with remaining colors.

3. Trace and transfer stencil patterns to folder; cut out. On chair back, stencil circle with yellow paint, using stencil brush; let dry. Center heart stencil over circle and stencil hearts, alternating dark pink, blue, and green paints (see photo). Randomly stencil light pink flowers and green leaves on chair. With small paintbrush, add dark pink centers to flowers; let dry. Outline flowers and leaves with colored pencil. To smooth paint, lightly sand chair.

4. Stack small piece of batting on top of large piece and center on chair seat. Center design piece over batting, folding ½" on all edges to back of batting. Attach to chair, using upholstery tacks.

Flower Stencil

Circle Stencil

Heart Stencil

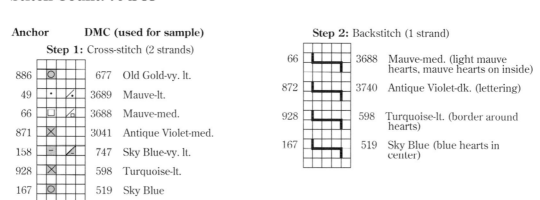

Stitch Count: 70 x 88

Anchor		DMC (used for sample)	
		Step 1: Cross-stitch (2 strands)	
886	◐	677	Old Gold-vy. lt.
49	· ╱	3689	Mauve-lt.
66	□ ╱	3688	Mauve-med.
871	✕	3041	Antique Violet-med.
158	− ╱	747	Sky Blue-vy. lt.
928	✕	598	Turquoise-lt.
167	◐	519	Sky Blue

Step 2: Backstitch (1 strand)

66		3688	Mauve-med. (light mauve hearts, mauve hearts on inside)
872		3740	Antique Violet-dk. (lettering)
928		598	Turquoise-lt. (border around hearts)
167		519	Sky Blue (blue hearts in center)

21

Presidents' Day

*The third Monday in February honors
all former presidents of the United States. Mark the
occasion with this cross-stitched trio of colonial motifs
reminiscent of our first leaders and the nation's
humble beginnings.*

Americana

SAMPLE
Stitched on white Linda 27 over 2 threads, the finished design size for Washington on Horseback and Hearts and Cat is 4⅛" x 3⅞" for each. The finished design size for Log Cabin is 4" x 3⅞". The fabric for each was cut 11" x 10". The designs are framed individually and mounted on a decorative shelf.

Washington on Horseback

FABRICS	DESIGN SIZES
Aida 11	5" x 4¾"
Aida 14	3⅞" x 3¾"
Aida 18	3" x 3"
Hardanger 22	2½" x 2⅜"

Hearts and Cat

FABRICS	DESIGN SIZES
Aida 11	5" x 4¾"
Aida 14	3⅞" x 3¾"
Aida 18	3" x 3"
Hardanger 22	2½" x 2⅜"

Log Cabin

FABRICS	DESIGN SIZES
Aida 11	4⅞" x 4¾"
Aida 14	3⅞" x 3¾"
Aida 18	3" x 2⅞"
Hardanger 22	2½" x 2⅜"

Anchor   DMC (used for sample)

Step 1: Cross-stitch (2 strands)

1		White
293	727	Topaz-vy. lt.
48	818	Baby Pink
24	776	Pink-med.
47	304	Christmas Red-med.
167	519	Sky Blue
132	797	Royal Blue
242	989	Forest Green
228	910	Emerald Green-dk.
882	407	Pecan
936	632	Pecan-dk.
401	844	Beaver Gray-ultra dk.

Step 2: Backstitch (1 strand)

370	434	Brown-lt. (sun)
401	844	Beaver Gray-ultra dk. (all else)

Step 3: French Knot (1 strand)

401	844	Beaver Gray-ultra dk.

Stitch Count: 55 x 53 (Washington on Horseback)

Anchor   DMC (used for sample)

Step 1: Cross-stitch (2 strands)

1		White
293	727	Topaz-vy. lt.
24	776	Pink-med.
47	304	Christmas Red-med.
167	519	Sky Blue
130	799	Delft-med.
132	797	Royal Blue
242	989	Forest Green
228	910	Emerald Green-dk.
882	407	Pecan
942	738	Tan-vy. lt.
362	437	Tan-lt.

Step 2: Backstitch (1 strand)

370	434	Brown-lt. (moon)
401	844	Beaver Gray-ultra dk. (all else)

Step 3: French Knot (1 strand)

401	844	Beaver Gray-ultra dk.

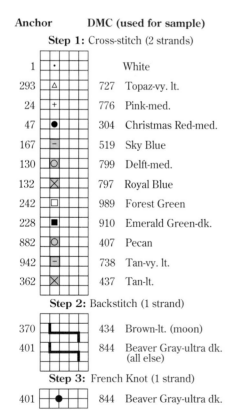

Stitch Count: 54 x 53 (Log Cabin)

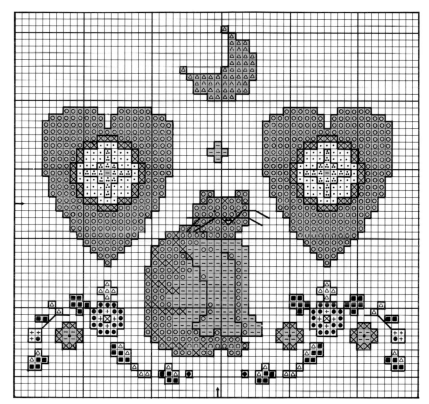

Stitch Count: 55 x 52 (Hearts and Cat)

Anchor		DMC (used for sample)

Step 1: Cross-stitch (2 strands)

Anchor	symbol	DMC	Name
1	·		White
293	△	727	Topaz-vy. lt.
24	+	776	Pink-med.
76	⊙	962	Wild Rose-med.
47	●	304	Christmas Red-med.
167	–	519	Sky Blue
130	⊠	799	Delft-med.
242	△	989	Forest Green
228	■	910	Emerald Green-dk.
942	–	738	Tan-vy. lt.
882	⊙	407	Pecan
936	⊠	632	Pecan-dk.
397	∴	453	Shell Gray-lt.
401	◢	844	Beaver Gray-ultra dk.

Step 2: Backstitch (1 strand)

Anchor		DMC	Name
370		434	Brown-lt. (moon)
401		844	Beaver Gray-ultra dk. (all else)

Step 3: French Knot (1 strand)

Anchor		DMC	Name
401	●	844	Beaver Gray-ultra dk.

National Pig Day

Pigs have become a popular theme for collectibles and design motifs. In honor of their special day, decorate with this clever wreath—it will be a guaranteed conversation piece!

For the Love of Pigs

SAMPLE
Stitched on white Aida 14 over 1 thread, finished design size is 2¾" x 2¾" for each. Fabric was cut 6" x 6" for each. Stitch 3.

FABRICS	DESIGN SIZES
Aida 11	3½" x 3½"
Aida 18	2⅛" x 2⅛"
Hardanger 22	1¾" x 1¾"

MATERIALS

3 completed cross-stitch designs on white Aida 14; matching thread

1 (4" x 24") piece of unstitched white Aida 14

¼ yard each of 2 (45"-wide) coordinating fabrics

⅛ yard (45"-wide) pink fabric for piping; matching thread

1 yard (⅛") cording

1¼ yards (1⁄16"-wide) white satin ribbon

1¼ yards (⅛"-wide) dusty rose satin ribbon

Stuffing

12" heart-shaped Styrofoam wreath

15" heart-shaped Styrofoam wreath

Assorted dried flowers

Hot-glue gun and glue sticks

Tracing paper

Dressmaker's pen

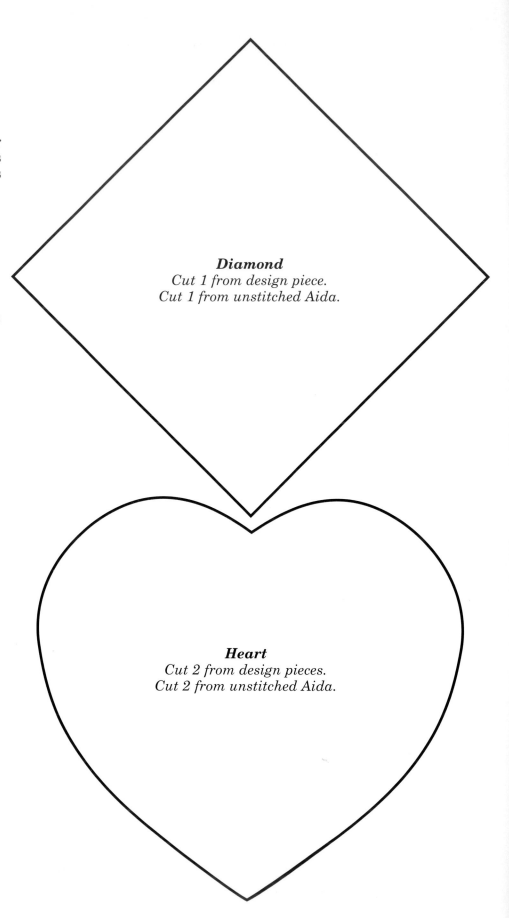

Diamond
Cut 1 from design piece.
Cut 1 from unstitched Aida.

Heart
Cut 2 from design pieces.
Cut 2 from unstitched Aida.

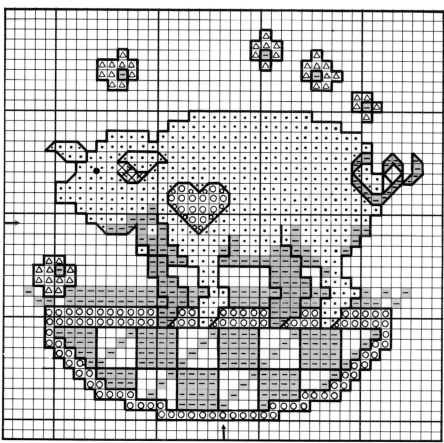

Stitch Count 39 x 38

Anchor			DMC	(used for sample)
			Step 1: Cross-stitch (2 strands)	
49	O	⊘	963	Wild Rose-vy. lt.
76	X	⊠	962	Wild Rose-med.
104	·	⟋	210	Lavender-med.
110	−	⟋	208	Lavender-vy. dk.
167	−		519	Sky Blue
215	△		320	Pistachio Green-med.
			Step 2: Backstitch (1 strand)	
149			311	Navy Blue-med.
			Step 3: French Knot (1 strand)	
149	●		311	Navy Blue-med.

DIRECTIONS

The patterns include ¼" seam allowances.

1. Make patterns. Center patterns on design pieces and cut out 1 diamond and 2 hearts. Also cut out 1 diamond and 2 hearts from unstitched Aida for backing.

2. From pink fabric, cut 1"-wide bias strips, piecing as needed to equal 1 yard. Make corded piping. Cut piping into 3 (12") lengths.

3. To make 1 ornament, with right sides facing and raw edges aligned, stitch 1 (12") length of piping to 1 design piece. With right sides facing and raw edges aligned, stitch design piece to matching backing piece, leaving an opening for turning. Trim corners and clip curves; turn. Stuff firmly. Slipstitch opening closed. Repeat to make remaining ornaments. Set aside.

4. Trim selvage from coordinating fabrics. For 12" heart, rip 1 fabric into 4 (1½"-wide) strips. For 15" heart, rip second fabric into 1 (4"-wide) strip and 4 (1½"-wide) strips. Set aside 1 (1½"-wide) strip from first fabric and 4"-wide strip from second fabric.

To cover 12" wreath, hot-glue 1 end of 1 strip to wreath and begin wrapping, pulling tightly. Allow edges of strip to overlap.

Secure end of strip with glue. Add additional strips until wreath is completely covered. Repeat for 15" heart.

5. To make ties, cut 1½"-wide strip that was set aside in half. Overlap wreaths slightly, with 12" heart on top (see photo). Tie hearts together tightly with fabric strips where wreaths overlap. Tie reserved 4"-wide strip in large bow around left side of 12" heart. Tie satin ribbons in bows around large fabric bow. Glue dried flowers to centers of bows. Tack design pieces to satin ribbon streamers.

Mountain Memories Weekend

When families relied on successful hunting as their primary means of survival, a sudden storm meant no meat on the table that night. Today, hunting is enjoyed primarily as a sport. The hill folk of Eastern Kentucky, however, keep the memory fresh by celebrating Mountain Memories Weekend with crafts, concerts, and storytelling. Another reminder is this piece depicting the ominous threat foul weather posed for the hunters of yesteryear.

The Hunt

SAMPLE

Stitched on cream Aida 14 over 1 thread, the finished design size is 8⅝" x 7⅛". The fabric was cut 15" x 14".

FABRICS	DESIGN SIZES
Aida 11	10⅞" x 9⅛"
Aida 18	6⅝" x 5½"
Hardanger 22	5½" x 4½"

Anchor		DMC (used for sample)	
Step 1: Cross-stitch (2 strands)			
1	+		White
300	E	745	Yellow-lt. pale
301	U	744	Yellow-pale
297	G	743	Yellow-med.
891	△	676	Old Gold-lt.
4146	S	754	Peach-lt.
868	╱	3779	Terra Cotta-vy. lt.
5968	●	355	Terra Cotta-dk.
9	H	760	Salmon
11	N	3328	Salmon-dk.
969	◨	3727	Antique Mauve-lt.
95	+	554	Violet-lt.
98	□	553	Violet-med.
99	∴	552	Violet-dk.
265	•	3348	Yellow Green-lt.

266	○	3347	Yellow Green-med.
257	U	3346	Hunter Green
185	– ╱	964	Seagreen-lt.
186	○	993	Aquamarine-lt.
187	✕ ╱	992	Aquamarine
188	∴	943	Aquamarine-med.
189	■	991	Aquamarine-dk.
849	I	927	Slate Green-med.
779	▽	926	Slate Green
851	✕	924	Slate Green-vy. dk.
347	• ╱	402	Mahogany-vy. lt.
308	○ ╲	976	Golden Brown-med.
355	U	975	Golden Brown-dk.
309	•	435	Brown-vy. lt.
371	+	433	Brown-med.
378	□	841	Beige Brown-lt.
379	▲	840	Beige Brown-med.
381	▽	938	Coffee Brown-ultra dk.
398	I	415	Pearl Gray
399	∴	318	Steel Gray-lt.
400	□	414	Steel Gray-dk.
401	✕ ╱	413	Pewter Gray-dk.
Step 2: Backstitch (1 strand)			
189		991	Aquamarine-dk. (trees)
381		938	Coffee Brown-ultra dk. (all else)

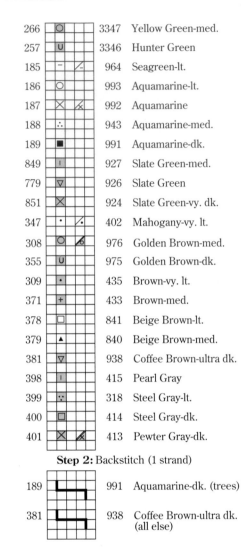
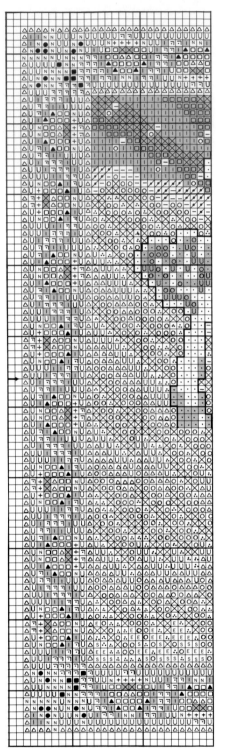

Stitch Count: 120 x 100

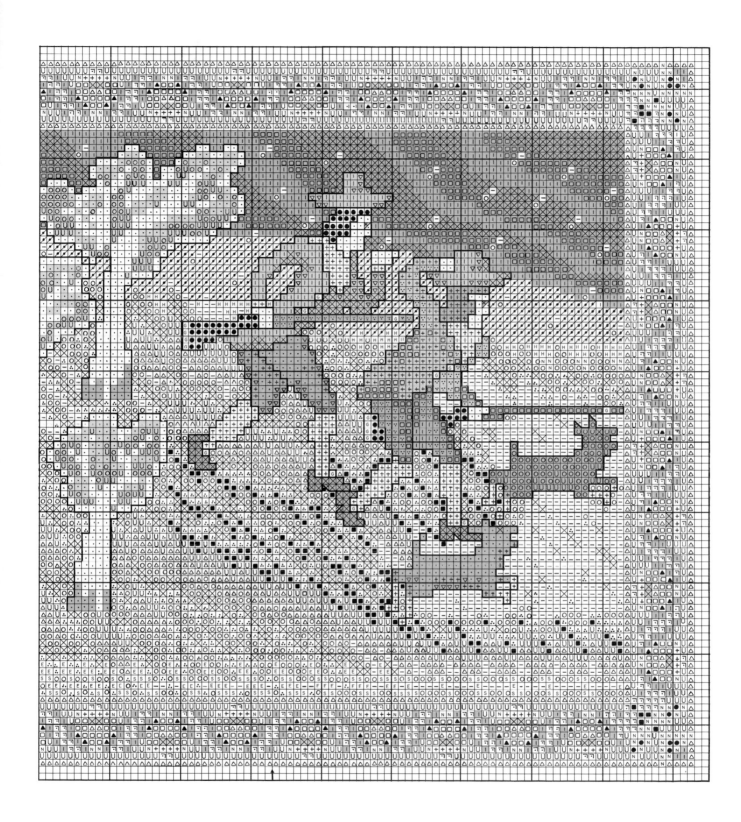

APRIL 6–13
Passover

*Passover is an
ancient Jewish festival
which celebrates the
Israelites' escape from
Egyptian slavery. Strict
dietary laws must be
followed, and work
is restricted at the
beginning and end of the
festival. Stitch this
traditional cloth for use
in observing Jewish holy
days as well as other
special family gatherings
when that extra touch
is sure to make
a difference.*

Star of David Cloth

SAMPLE

Stitched on white Belfast Linen 32 over 2 threads, the finished design size is 19⅞" x 19⅞". The fabric was cut 22½" x 22½". Begin stitching corner leaf in the bottom right corner, 1¼" from each edge of the fabric, according to the graph. Complete 2 repeats and rotate graph clockwise a ¼ turn. Repeat to complete cloth.

FABRICS	DESIGN SIZES
Aida 11	29" x 29"
Aida 14	22¾" x 22¾"
Aida 18	17¾" x 17¾"
Hardanger 22	14½" x 14½"

MATERIALS

Completed cross-stitch on white Belfast Linen 32; matching thread
2¾ yards (2"-wide) white scalloped lace

DIRECTIONS

1. To hem cloth, fold raw edges of linen under ⅛" twice to back. Slipstitch, mitering corners.

2. Slipstitch straight edge of lace to right side of hemmed edges of runner, pleating lace at each corner to fit.

Anchor		DMC (used for sample)	
		Step 1: Cross-stitch (2 strands)	
891	○	676	Old Gold-lt.
66	✕	3688	Mauve-med.
95	○	554	Violet-lt.
118	✕	340	Blue Violet-med.
842	□	3013	Khaki Green-lt.
859	■	3052	Green Gray-med.

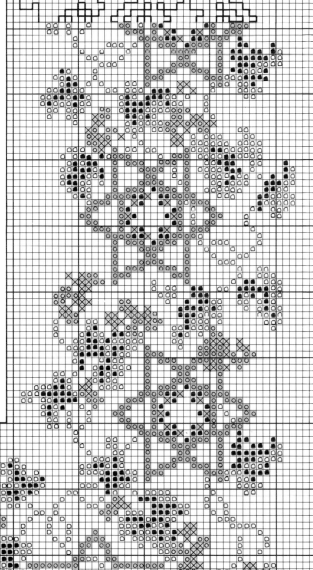

Stitch Count: 319 x 319 (entire design)

Repeat

APRIL 11
Easter

Dressed in dapper tweed and polished cotton, sporting jaunty hats and cross-stitched accessories, these dolled-up bunnies are ready for the Easter parade. And judging from their looks, they plan to have a "hare"-raising time!

Face: Paint shaded area white. Paint nose pink. Use black marker to outline facial features and fill in eyes.

Bunny Buddies

SAMPLE

Stitched on apricot Pastel Linen 28 over 2 threads, the finished design size is 1⅛" x 2⅝" for the necktie and 5¼" x 2⅝" for the apron. The fabric was cut 4" x 7" for the necktie. See Step 1 of apron directions before cutting apron.

Necktie

FABRICS	DESIGN SIZES
Aida 11	1⅜" x 3⅜"
Aida 14	1⅛" x 2⅝"
Aida 18	⅞" x 2"
Hardanger 22	⅝" x 1⅝"

Apron

FABRICS	DESIGN SIZES
Aida 11	6⅝" x 3⅜"
Aida 14	5¼" x 2⅝"
Aida 18	4" x 2"
Hardanger 22	3⅜" x 1⅝"

MATERIALS (for 1 bunny)

½ yard (45"-wide) white polished cotton; matching thread
Stuffing
28" of florist's wire, cut in half
Acrylic paints: white, light pink
Small paintbrush
Fine-tip permanent black marker
1 (7"-wide) natural or white straw hat
Polyester "silk" flowers for girl bunny (optional)
Tracing paper
Dressmaker's pen

DIRECTIONS

The patterns include ¼" seam allowances.

1. Make patterns for body, ears, and legs. Transfer patterns to fabric and cut out.

2. With right sides facing and raw edges aligned, stitch 2 ear pieces together, leaving straight edge open. Clip curves; turn. Fold 1 piece of wire in half; curve to match shape of ear. Insert in ear. Repeat for other ear. Make a ¼" tuck on straight raw edge of each ear; baste. Baste ears to right side of 1 body piece (see pattern for placement). With right sides facing and raw edges aligned, stitch body pieces together, securing tucked edges of ears in seam and leaving bottom edge of body open. Clip curves; turn. Stuff arms and body firmly to within ½" of bottom raw edge. Topstitch arms through all layers where indicated on pattern.

3. With right sides facing and raw edges aligned, stitch 2 leg pieces together, leaving straight edge open. Clip curves; turn. Stuff firmly to within ½" of top raw edge. Repeat for other leg. With right sides facing, raw edges aligned, and leg seams centered at front and back, stitch straight edges of legs to bottom edge of body front so that toes will face forward (see pattern for placement). Slipstitch opening closed.

4. For face, make pattern and cut out. Transfer facial features from pattern to fabric. Referring to pattern, paint shaded area of pattern white. Let dry. Paint nose pink. Let dry. Using fine-tip permanent black marker, trace remaining facial features and fill in eyes. Add white highlight to eyes with a dot of white paint.

For girl bunny, decorate hat with flowers as desired. To attach hat to girl or boy bunny, cut 2 (1") slits, 1" apart and 1½" from crown. Pull ears through slits and position as desired.

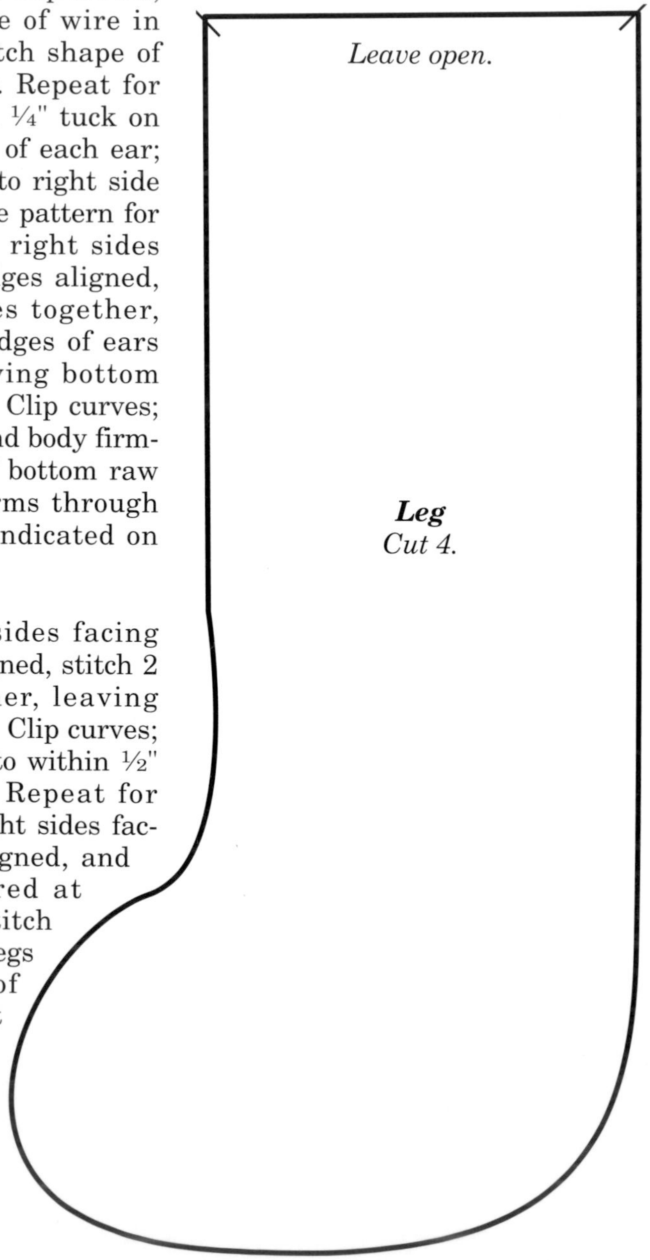

Leave open.

Leg
Cut 4.

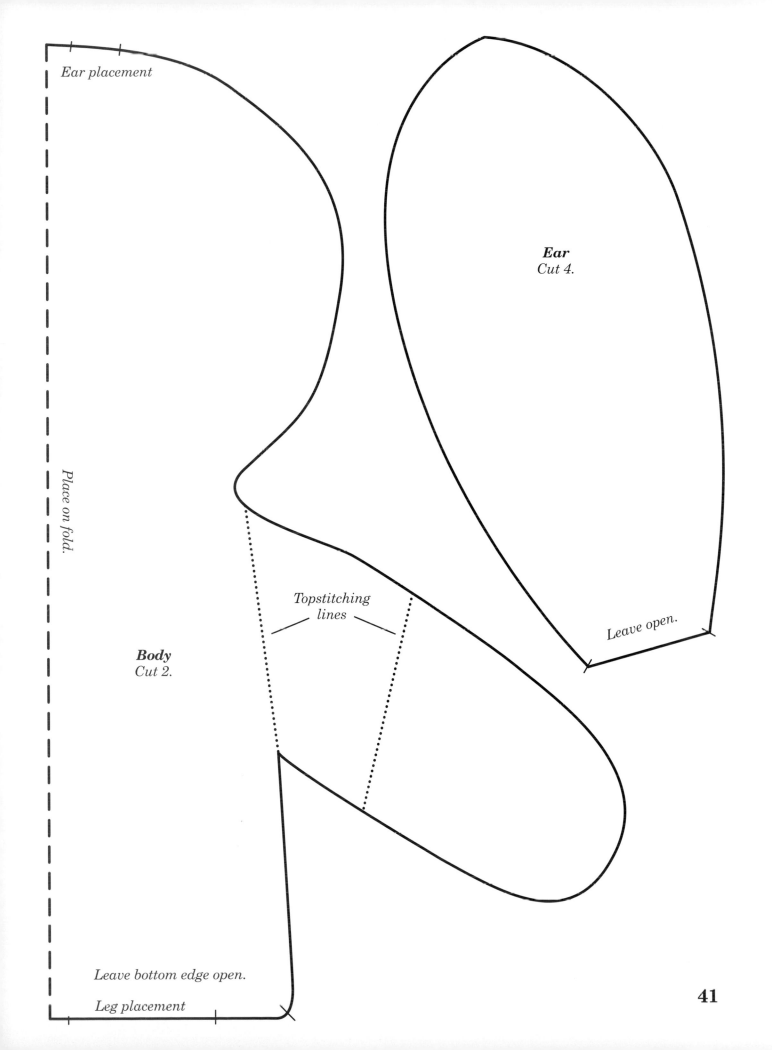

Ear placement

Place on fold.

Ear
Cut 4.

Leave open.

Topstitching
lines

Body
Cut 2.

Leave bottom edge open.

Leg placement

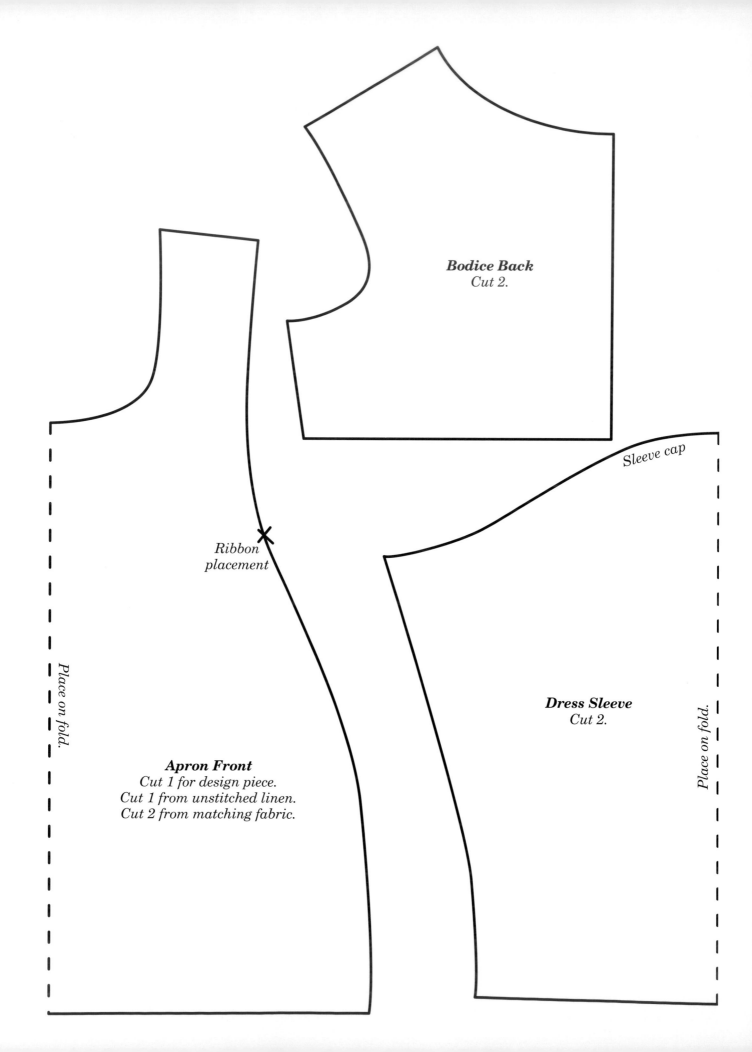

Bodice Back
Cut 2.

Sleeve cap

Ribbon placement

Place on fold.

Dress Sleeve
Cut 2.

Place on fold.

Apron Front
Cut 1 for design piece.
Cut 1 from unstitched linen.
Cut 2 from matching fabric.

MATERIALS for Dress

½ yard (45"-wide) aqua polished cotton; matching thread

¼ yard (⅛"-wide) elastic, cut in half

3 small snap sets

DIRECTIONS

The patterns include ¼" seam allowances.

1. Make patterns for bodice front, bodice back, and sleeve. Transfer patterns to fabric and cut out. Cut 1 (8" x 24") piece for skirt. From remaining fabric, cut ¾"-wide bias strips, piecing as needed to equal 10" for neck binding.

2. With right sides facing and raw edges aligned, stitch bodice front to bodice backs at shoulders. With right sides facing and raw edges aligned, stitch 1 edge of bias strip along neckline. Fold bias strip over raw edge to back, turn under ¼", and slipstitch. Turn under ¼" on each center back edge of bodice for opening and press.

3. Run a gathering thread along raw edge of 1 sleeve cap. Pull thread to gather to fit armhole. With right sides facing and raw edges aligned, stitch sleeve cap to bodice. Repeat for other sleeve. With right sides of bodice and sleeve facing and raw edges aligned, stitch 1 underarm/side seam. Repeat for remaining side. Fold straight edge of 1 sleeve under ¼" twice to make casing. Stitch through all layers as close to first folded edge as possible, leaving a small opening. Thread elastic through casing. Overlap ends of elastic and secure. Stitch opening closed. Repeat for other sleeve.

4. To make skirt, with right sides facing and raw edges aligned, fold skirt in half, matching short edges. Stitch short raw edges together to within 2" of 1 end; backstitch. Press seam open. (This seam is center back; end with opening is waist edge.) To hem bottom edge of skirt, fold fabric under 1½"; then fold raw edge under ½" and slipstitch in place. Run a gathering thread along raw edge of skirt waist. Pull to gather to fit bodice. With right sides facing and raw edges aligned, stitch gathered edge of skirt to bodice, matching center back openings and seam. Zigzag raw edges of all seam allowances around waist. Fold center back edges ½" to inside. Sew snaps on center back opening of bodice.

Place on fold.

Bodice Front
Cut 1.

MATERIALS for Apron

¼ yard of apricot Pastel Linen 28; matching thread

¼ yard (45"-wide) matching apricot fabric for lining

1¼ yards (¼"-wide) matching satin ribbon

Dressmaker's pen

DIRECTIONS

The pattern includes ¼" seam allowance.

1. Make apron pattern. Transfer pattern to linen with dressmaker's pen. Center and work cross-stitch design across fabric, with bottom of design ½" from bottom edge of traced outline. Cut out.

2. From remaining unstitched linen, cut 1 apron back. Cut 2 apron pieces from matching fabric for lining. Cut ribbon into 4 equal lengths.

3. On right side of design piece, with raw edges of ribbons and apron piece aligned, baste 1 end of 1 ribbon to each side (see pattern for placement). Repeat for apron back. With right sides facing and raw edges aligned, stitch design piece and 1 lining piece together along sides and bottom, securing ribbons in seams and leaving neck and shoulders open. Repeat for apron back. Trim corners and clip curves. Turn. Slipstitch front and back neck and shoulder openings closed. Match front and back shoulder straps on each side. Slipstitch together.

43

MATERIALS for Necktie and Shirt

Completed cross-stitch on apricot Pastel Linen 28; matching thread
Scrap of unstitched apricot Pastel Linen 28 for neck band
Scrap of matching apricot fabric for lining
⅛ yard (45"-wide) white fabric; matching thread
Scrap of fusible interfacing
3 (⅜") white buttons
1 small snap set

DIRECTIONS

The patterns include ¼" seam allowances.

1. Make patterns for shirt front, back, sleeve, shirt collar, and necktie. Center necktie pattern on design piece; cut out. Also cut 1 each from matching fabric and fusible interfacing. From unstitched linen, cut 1 (1¼" x 9") strip for neck band. Cut shirt pieces from white fabric.

2. For necktie, fuse interfacing to wrong side of design piece, following manufacturer's directions. With right sides facing and raw edges aligned, stitch design piece and lining piece together, leaving an opening at top and 1½" along 1 side. Trim corners; turn. Slipstitch opening closed. Set aside. With right sides facing and long raw edges aligned, fold neck band in half lengthwise. Stitch long edges together; turn. Slipstitch openings closed. Fold top side edges of design piece to center back; baste. Centering neck band on top of necktie, pinch band around top of necktie and tack through all layers to resemble a knot. Sew snap to ends of neck band. Set aside.

3. For collar, with right sides facing and raw edges aligned, stitch pieces together, leaving straight edge open. Clip curves, turn, and press.

4. With right sides facing and raw edges aligned, stitch front pieces to back at shoulders. With raw edges aligned, baste collar to right side of neckline between dots. Zigzag raw edges of self facing on fronts. With right sides facing and raw edges aligned, fold each self facing toward shirt front along fold line (see pattern). Stitch around neckline through all layers of facings and collar. Zigzag seam allowances of neck and bottom edges of fronts and back. Turn facings right side out. Slipstitch facings to inside of shirt.

5. Zigzag straight raw edges of sleeve; fold each edge ½" to back and stitch hem. With right sides facing and raw edges aligned, stitch sleeve caps to armholes, easing sleeves as needed. With right sides facing and raw edges aligned, stitch 1 underarm/side seam. Repeat for remaining side. Fold zigzagged bottom edge of shirt under ¼" once and slipstitch hem in place.

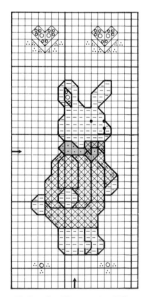

Stitch Count: 15 x 37 (Necktie)

Stitch Count: 73 x 37 (Apron)

6. Make ½" buttonholes on left edge of shirt front (see pattern for placement). Sew buttons on right edge.

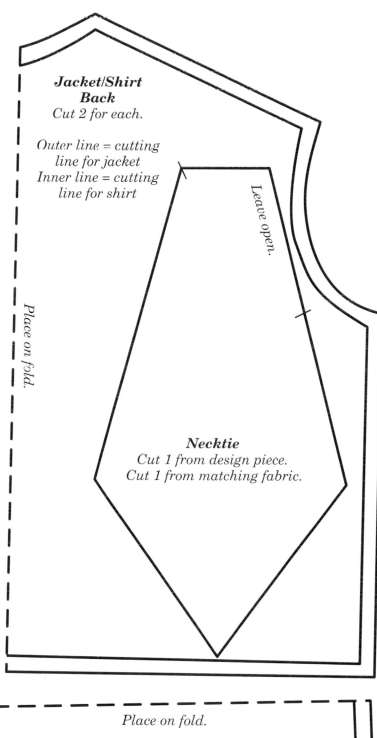

Jacket/Shirt Back
Cut 2 for each.

Outer line = cutting line for jacket
Inner line = cutting line for shirt

Leave open.

Place on fold.

Necktie
Cut 1 from design piece.
Cut 1 from matching fabric.

Leave open.

Place on fold.

Shirt Collar
Cut 2.

Place on fold.

Jacket/Shirt Sleeve
Cut 2 for each.

Outer line = cutting line for jacket
Inner line = cutting line for shirt

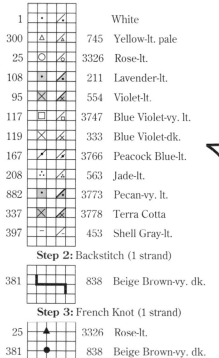

Anchor			DMC	(used for sample)

Step 1: Cross-stitch (2 strands)

1	·	⁄		White
300	△	⁄	745	Yellow-lt. pale
25	○	⁄	3326	Rose-lt.
108	·	⁄	211	Lavender-lt.
95	✕	⁄	554	Violet-lt.
117	□	⁄	3747	Blue Violet-vy. lt.
119	✕	⁄	333	Blue Violet-dk.
167	⁄	⁄	3766	Peacock Blue-lt.
208	∴	⁄	563	Jade-lt.
882	·	⁄	3773	Pecan-vy. lt.
337	✕	⁄	3778	Terra Cotta
397	–	⁄	453	Shell Gray-lt.

Step 2: Backstitch (1 strand)

381		838	Beige Brown-vy. dk.

Step 3: French Knot (1 strand)

25	▲	3326	Rose-lt.
381	●	838	Beige Brown-vy. dk.

45

MATERIALS for Jacket

⅛ yard (45"-wide) gray wool tweed; matching thread
Scrap of gray polyester for collar lining
1 (½") gray button

DIRECTIONS

The patterns include ¼" seam allowances.

1. Make patterns for jacket front, back, sleeve, and jacket collar. Transfer patterns to fabrics and cut out.

2. With right sides facing and raw edges aligned, stitch collar pieces together, leaving straight edge open. Clip curves, turn, and press.

3. To assemble jacket, refer to Steps 4 and 5 of shirt directions.

4. Make ⅝" buttonhole on left edge of jacket front (see pattern for placement). Sew button on right edge. To make lapels, fold facings back toward jacket fronts.

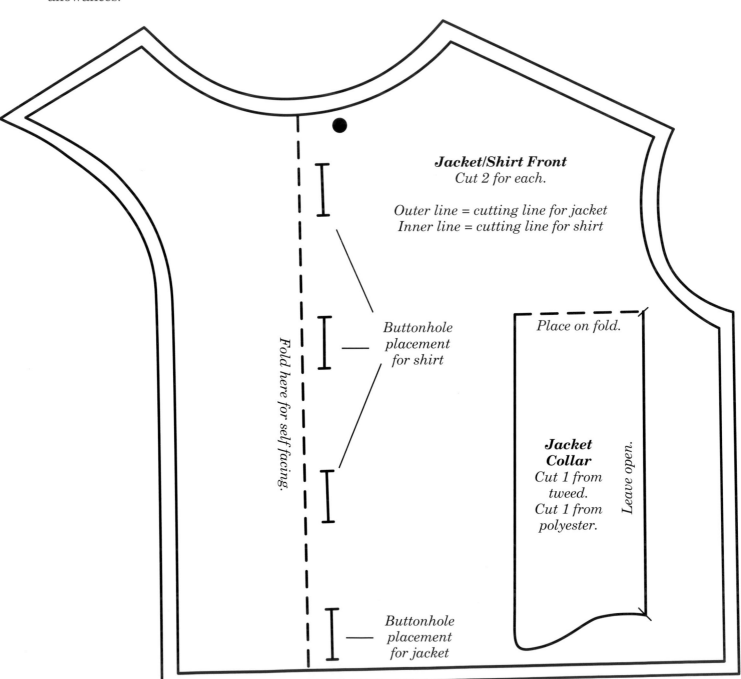

Jacket/Shirt Front
Cut 2 for each.

Outer line = cutting line for jacket
Inner line = cutting line for shirt

Buttonhole placement for shirt

Fold here for self facing.

Place on fold.

Leave open.

Jacket Collar
Cut 1 from tweed.
Cut 1 from polyester.

Buttonhole placement for jacket

MATERIALS for Pants

Scrap of gray wool; matching thread

¼ yard (¼"-wide) elastic

DIRECTIONS

The pattern includes ¼" seam allowance.

1. Make pants pattern. Transfer pattern to fabric and cut out.

2. Zigzag bottom raw edge of each pants leg. Fold edges under ½" once; stitch hem. With right sides facing and raw edges aligned, stitch inseam on each pants leg. Turn 1 pants leg right side out; place inside other leg so that right sides are facing and inseams are matching. With raw edges aligned, stitch center front and back seam (see Diagram). Turn pants. To make waistband casing, zigzag raw edge of waist and fold edge under ½". Stitch waistband close to zigzagged edge, leaving an opening. Thread elastic through casing. Overlap ends of elastic ½" and secure. Stitch opening closed.

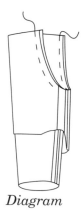

Diagram

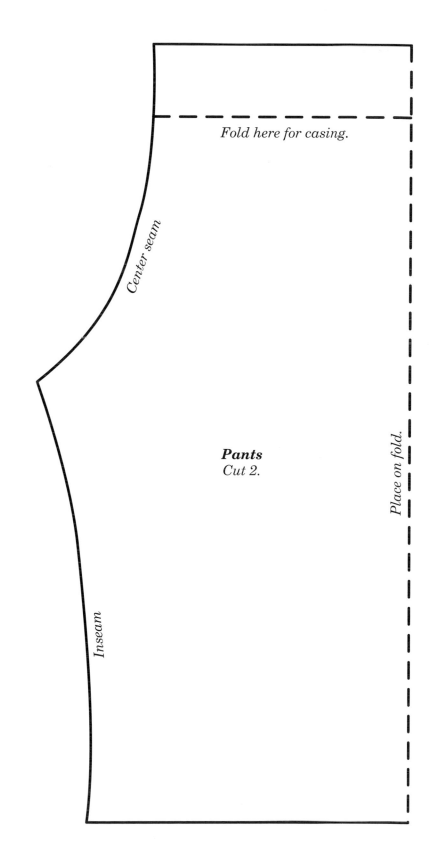

Fold here for casing.

Center seam

Inseam

Pants
Cut 2.

Place on fold.

National Wildlife Week

Bears have appeared in legends and folktales for centuries. Once hunted until they were nearly extinct, these huge animals are now a protected species. This cross-stitched version of Ursus horribilis *would make a great addition to Dad's den as the perfect representative of National Wildlife Week.*

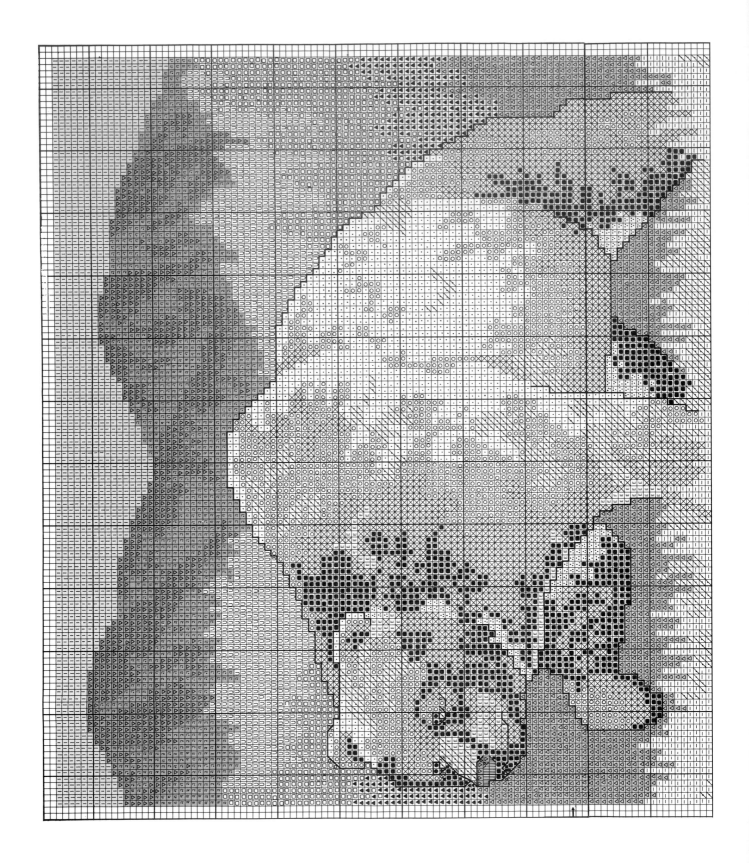

50

Stitch Count: 120 x 167

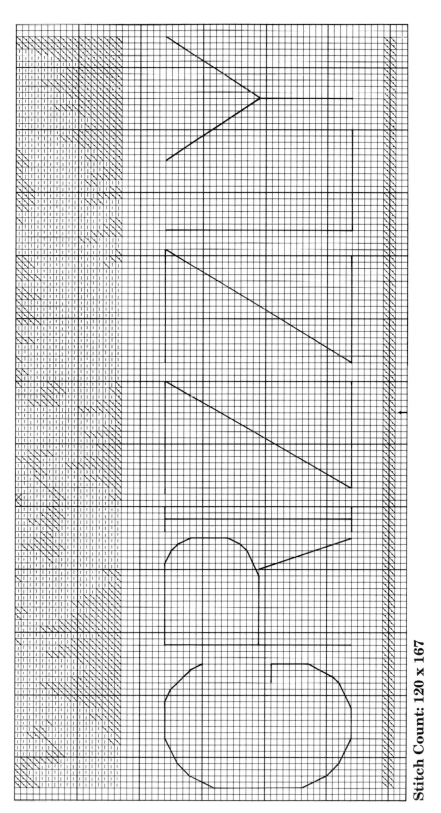

Grizzly

SAMPLE

Stitched on Rustico 14 over 1 thread, the finished design size is 8⅝" x 11⅞". The fabric was cut 15" x 18". See Suppliers for material.

FABRICS	**DESIGN SIZES**
Aida 11	10⅞" x 15⅛"
Aida 14	8⅝" x 11⅞"
Aida 18	6⅝" x 9¼"
Hardanger 22	5½" x 7⅝"

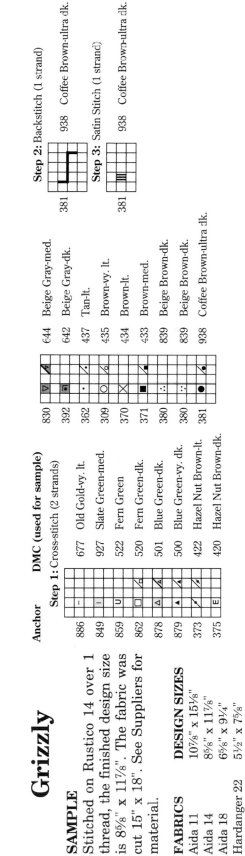

Anchor			DMC (used for sample)	
	Step 1: Cross-stitch (2 strands)			
886	–		677	Old Gold-vy. lt.
849	I		927	Slate Green-med.
859	U		522	Fern Green
862	□	◿	520	Fern Green-dk.
878	△	◿	501	Blue Green-dk.
879	▲	◿	500	Blue Green-vy. dk.
373	⁄	⁄	422	Hazel Nut Brown-lt.
375	E		420	Hazel Nut Brown-dk.
830	▽	◿	644	Beige Gray-med.
392	▪		642	Beige Gray-dk.
362	•	⁄	437	Tan-lt.
309	○	⁄	435	Brown-vy. lt.
370	╳		434	Brown-lt.
371	■	⁄	433	Brown-med.
380	∴		839	Beige Brown-dk.
380	∵		839	Beige Brown-dk.
381	●	⁄	938	Coffee Brown-ultra dk.
	Step 2: Backstitch (1 strand)			
381			938	Coffee Brown-ultra dk.
	Step 3: Satin Stitch (1 strand)			
381			938	Coffee Brown-ultra dk.

Earth Day Anniversary

Since the first celebration of Earth Day in 1970, citizens of the world have begun to reclaim the air, water, and living environment. This tribute to Mother Earth's bounty is an annual event, dedicated to the preservation of these precious resources. A new appreciation for what we have requires a new commitment to renew, recycle, and restore.

For we must share
if we would keep
That blessing
from above:
Ceasing to give,
we cease to have,
Such is the law
of love.

Earth Awareness

SAMPLE

Stitched on cream Jobelan 28 over 2 threads, the finished design size is 11⅞" x 16½". The fabric was cut 18" x 23". See Suppliers for material.

FABRICS   **DESIGN SIZES**

Aida 11   15⅛" x 21"
Aida 14   11⅞" x 16½"
Aida 18   9¼" x 12⅞"
Hardanger 22   7½" x 10½"

Anchor	DMC (used for sample)

Step 1: Cross-stitch (2 strands)

851	924	Slate Green-vy. dk.

Step 2: Backstitch (1 strand)

851	924	Slate Green-vy. dk.

Step 3: French Knot (1 strand)

851	924	Slate Green-vy. dk.

For we must share
If we would keep
That blessing
from above:
Ceasing to give,
we cease to have,
Such is the law
of love.

MAY

National Home Decorating Month

Small details contribute to the overall decor of your home, inviting friends to take note of your personal style. These dainty chairs and cushions are a welcome addition to any nook or cranny.

Miniature Cushions

SAMPLE
Stitched on Linaida 14 over 1 thread, finished design size is 3¼" x 3¼" for each. Fabric was cut 10" x 10" for each. See Suppliers for material.

FABRICS	DESIGN SIZES
Aida 11	4⅛" x 4⅛"
Aida 14	3¼" x 3¼"
Aida 18	2½" x 2½"
Hardanger 22	2" x 2"

MATERIALS (for 1 chair)
Completed cross-stitch on Linaida 14; matching thread
Scrap of unstitched Linaida 14 for back
Scrap of cotton fabric: dusty rose for pink cushion or pine green for violet cushion
½ yard (⅛") cording
Stuffing
1 purchased high-back wooden doll chair with 4½"-square seat (available at craft stores)
Acrylic paint coordinated with fabric
Paintbrush

DIRECTIONS
All seam allowances are ¼".

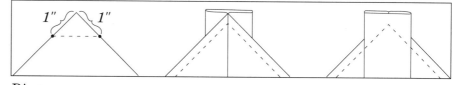

Diagram

1. With design centered, trim design piece to 6" square. From unstitched Linaida, cut a 6" square for back. From cotton fabric, cut 1"-wide bias strips, piecing as needed to make ½ yard. Make corded piping.

2. To make pleated corners, measure 1" on adjacent edges of 1 corner of design piece and mark. Referring to Diagram, cut diagonally from point to point across corner. Make a

pleat by folding sides to center as indicated; baste in place. Repeat for remaining corners of cushion front and for each corner of cushion back.

3. To attach piping, with right sides facing and raw edges aligned, stitch piping to design piece, slightly rounding corners and catching pleats in seam. With right sides facing and raw edges aligned, stitch design piece to cushion back,

sewing along stitching line of piping and leaving an opening for turning. Trim corners and turn. Stuff moderately. Slipstitch opening closed.

4. Paint chair and allow to dry before putting cushion in place.

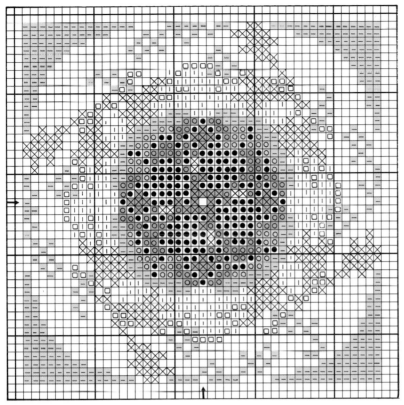

Stitch Count: 45 x 45 (Pink)

Anchor		DMC	(used for sample)
		Step 1:	Cross-stitch (2 strands)
868	□	758	Terra Cotta-lt.
896	⊠	3721	Shell Pink-dk.
968	I	778	Antique Mauve vy. lt.
969	◎	316	Antique Mauve-med.
920	–	932	Antique Blue-lt.
921	○	931	Antique Blue-med.
843	⊠	3364	Pine Green
861	●	3363	Pine Green-med.

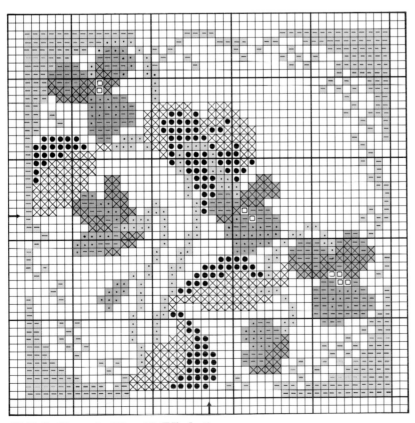

Stitch Count: 46 x 46 (Violet)

Anchor		DMC	(used for sample)
		Step 1:	Cross-stitch (2 strands)
300	□	745	Yellow-lt. pale
95	·	554	Violet-lt. (1 strand) +
871		3041	Antique Violet-med. (1 strand)
871	▬	3041	Antique Violet-med.
101	⊠	327	Antique Violet-vy. dk.
920	–	932	Antique Blue-lt.
843	·	3364	Pine Green
861	⊠	3363	Pine Green-med.
862	●	520	Fern Green-dk.

59

MAY 7-9
Wildflower Weekend

Wrap yourself in some of Mother Nature's finest foliage with this cozy wildflower afghan. These blossoms are also the focus of a weekend of activities at Natural Bridge Resort State Park in Slade, Kentucky.

Wildflowers in Bloom

SAMPLE
Stitched on Vanessa-Ann Afghan Weave 18 over 2 threads. Fabric was cut 48" x 58" (width measurement includes 7 whole blocks and ½ block on each side; length measurement includes 8 whole blocks and ½ block at top and bottom). Stitching area of each woven block is 88 x 88 threads. The heavy black lines surrounding each graph indicate the block boundaries. Begin stitching in lower lefthand whole block of afghan, following Diagram A for placement of designs. See Suppliers for afghan material.

MATERIALS
Completed cross-stitch on Vanessa-Ann Afghan Weave 18; matching thread

Filatura Di Crosa yarn, 3 skeins Sympathie #934 (see Suppliers)
Large-eyed needle

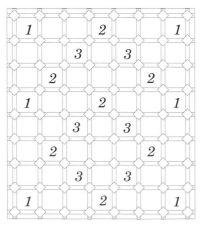

Diagram A

DIRECTIONS
1. To hem afghan, fold top and bottom selvage edges under once to back; slipstitch. Fold raw side edges under ¾" twice to back. Slipstitch, mitering corners.

2. On top and bottom edges, mark center of each diamond shape in decorative weave. Fanpleat in 3 equal folds distance between center of each diamond and corresponding hemmed edge. Using matching thread, tack folds securely through center of each diamond.

3. To make tassels for fringe: For each tassel, cut 16 (36"), 1 (10"), and 1 (30") pieces of yarn. Handling 36" lengths as 1, fold yarn in half. Fold 10" length of yarn in half and tie around tassel fold for yarn tie; knot close to fold (see Diagram B). Referring to Diagrams B, C, and D, wrap 30" piece of yarn ½" below fold; secure ends and tuck into tassels. Repeat to make 16 tassels.

On 1 end of afghan, attach 1 tassel to each gathered section of fan pleats, threading yarn tie through all folds (see Diagram E). Repeat with remaining 8 tassels across other end.

4. Place afghan on large, flat surface so all tassels are easily accessible. To make knotted fringe, divide strands of each tassel in half. Join half of 1 tassel to half of adjacent tassel in a square knot 3" from yarn wrap (see Diagram F). Repeat across each end.

5. Divide new tassels in half. Again join adjacent halves together in square knots, 3" from previous knot (see Diagram G). Repeat across each end.

6. To make 14 additional tassels: For each tassel, cut 16 (18") and 1 (30") pieces of yarn. Handling 18" lengths as 1, fold yarn in half over 1 square knot in first row. Wrap 30" piece of yarn around strands, ½" below fold (see Diagram H). Secure ends and tuck into tassels. Repeat across each end.

7. Spread out all tassels so they are straight and parallel. Trim evenly to make 12"-deep fringe.

Diagram B

Diagram C

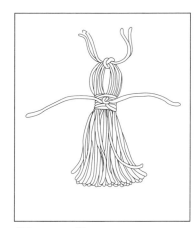

Diagram D

Diagram E

Diagram F

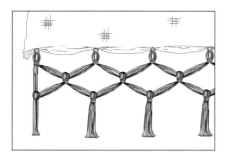

Diagram G

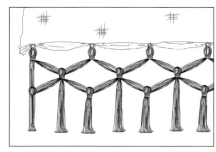

Diagram H

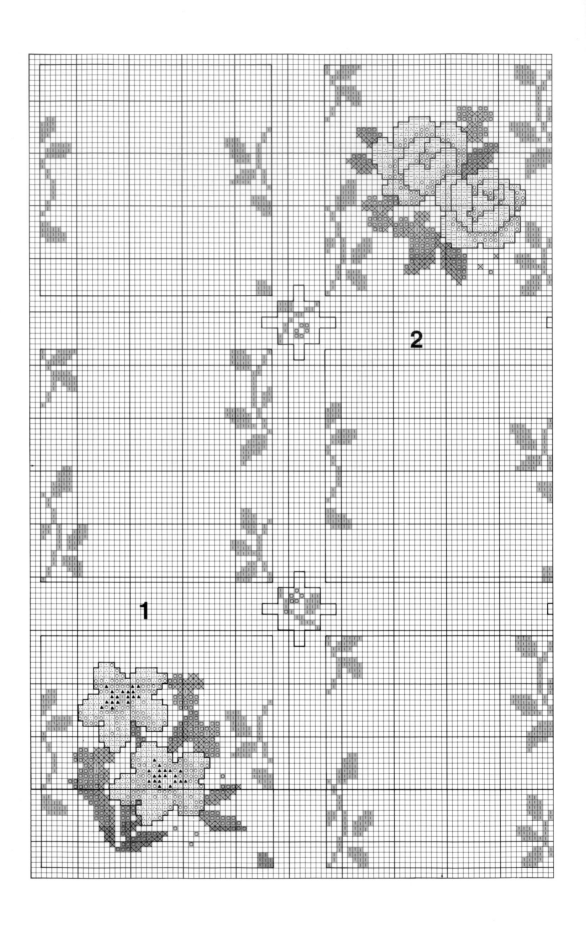

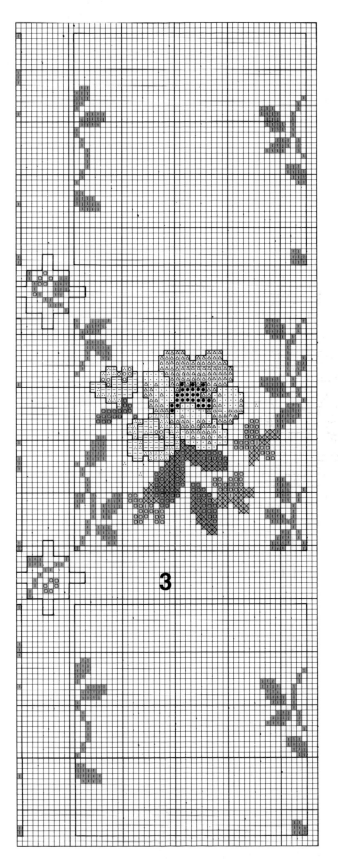

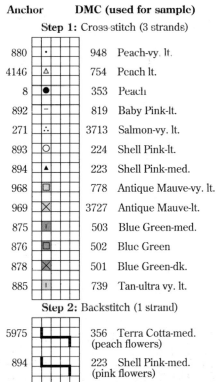

Anchor		DMC (used for sample)	
Step 1: Cross-stitch (3 strands)			
880	·	948	Peach-vy. lt.
4146	△	754	Peach lt.
8	●	353	Peach
892	–	819	Baby Pink-lt.
271	∴	3713	Salmon-vy. lt.
893	○	224	Shell Pink-lt.
894	▲	223	Shell Pink-med.
968	▢	778	Antique Mauve-vy. lt.
969	⨯	3727	Antique Mauve-lt.
875	▦	503	Blue Green-med.
876	▢	502	Blue Green
878	⨯	501	Blue Green-dk.
885	▯	739	Tan-ultra vy. lt.
Step 2: Backstitch (1 strand)			
5975		356	Terra Cotta-med. (peach flowers)
894		223	Shell Pink-med. (pink flowers)

3

Mother's Day

*For all the care and affection that Mother
shares throughout the year, this day is the perfect time
to return these sentiments with a gift made especially for
her loving hands. Each of these pretty tea towels,
embellished with floral borders and an appliquéd heart,
is a tribute to Mother's abiding devotion.*

Hearts & Flowers Tea Towels

SAMPLE for Mauve Border
Stitched on a 17" x 24½" purchased tea towel using Waste Canvas 14, the finished design size is 3¾" x 2" for 1 motif. The canvas was cut 17" x 4". Begin stitching border 3" from the bottom and 1" from 1 side of towel. Repeat motif 4 times.

FABRICS	DESIGN SIZES
Aida 11	4¾" x 2½"
Aida 14	3¾" x 2"
Aida 18	3" x 1½"
Hardanger 22	2⅜" x 1¼"

SAMPLE for Purple Border
Stitched on a 17" x 24½" purchased tea towel using Waste Canvas 14, the finished design size is 3¾" x 2⅛" for 1 motif. The canvas was cut 5" x 4". Fold canvas and tea towel in half to find vertical center of each. Match centers and begin stitching border 3" from the bottom.

FABRICS	DESIGN SIZES
Aida 11	4¾" x 2⅝"
Aida 14	3¾" x 2⅛"
Aida 18	3" x 1⅝"
Hardanger 22	2⅜" x 1⅜"

SAMPLE for Hearts
Stitched on cream Belfast Linen 32 over 2 threads, each finished design size is 2¾" x 2⅝". The fabric was cut 6" x 6" for each. Stitch 1 for each towel.

FABRICS	DESIGN SIZES
Aida 11	4⅛" x 3⅞"
Aida 14	3¼" x 3"
Aida 18	2½" x 2⅜"
Hardanger 22	2" x 1⅞"

MATERIALS (for 1 tea towel)
Completed cross-stitch on purchased tea towel (see Sample information)
Completed cross-stitch heart on cream Belfast Linen 32; matching thread

DIRECTIONS
1. Trim design piece to within ½" of heart-shaped design. Center heart ¾" above border. Turn raw edge under ¼" and appliqué to towel.

2. Outline-quilt along inside and outside edges of cross-stitched heart shape.

DMC (used for sample)

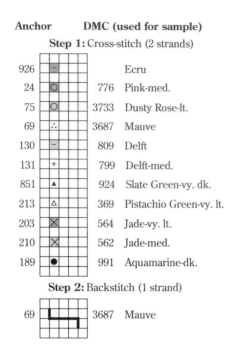

Step 1: Cross-stitch (2 strands)

926	–	Ecru
24	⊙	776	Pink-med.
75	⊙	3733	Dusty Rose-lt.
69	∴	3687	Mauve
130	–	809	Delft
131	+	799	Delft-med.
851	▲	924	Slate Green-vy. dk.
213	△	369	Pistachio Green-vy. lt.
203	⊠	564	Jade-vy. lt.
210	⊠	562	Jade-med.
189	●	991	Aquamarine-dk.

Step 2: Backstitch (1 strand)

| 69 | | 3687 | Mauve |

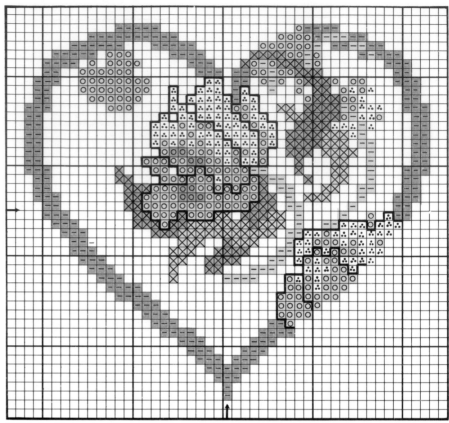

Stitch Count: 45 x 42 (for 1 Mauve Heart Motif)

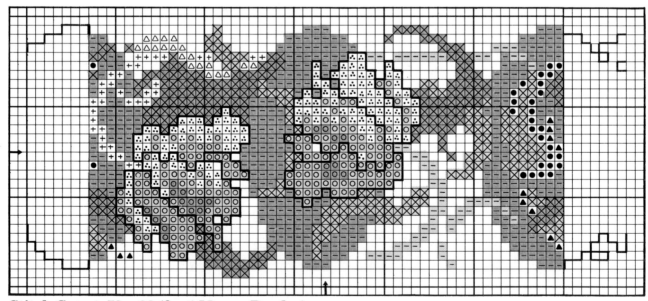

Stitch Count: 53 x 28 (for 1 Mauve Border)

Anchor   **DMC** (used for sample)

Step 1: Cross-stitch (2 strands)

Anchor		DMC	
300	△	745	Yellow-lt. pale
4146	· ╱	754	Peach-lt.
75	▬	3733	Dusty Rose-lt.
104	○ ╱	210	Lavender-med.
101	●	327	Antique Violet-vy. dk.
168	▬	807	Peacock Blue
186	⊠	993	Aquamarine-lt.
189	✕	991	Aquamarine-dk.
265	■	3348	Yellow Green-lt.

Step 2: Backstitch (1 strand)

101	⌐_	327	Antique Violet-vy. dk. (flowers)
189	⌐_	991	Aquamarine-dk. (veins in leaves)

Stitch Count: 45 x 42 (for 1 Purple Heart Motif)

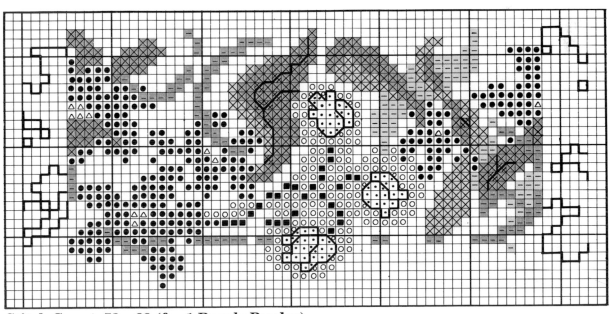

Stitch Count: 53 x 29 (for 1 Purple Border)

JUNE

National Adopt-a-Cat Month

In spite of their affectionate nature, many cats are homeless. June has been designated the month to adopt these forgotten felines. Whether your place is an apartment or a mansion, consider adding a cat to make it truly a home.

The "Purrfect" Wall Hanging

SAMPLE

Stitched on Waste Canvas 14 over 1 thread, the finished design size for each corner motif is 2⅞" x 2⅞". The canvas and fabric were cut 5" x 5" for 1 motif. Stitch 4. The finished design size for 1 border motif is 2¼" x 3⅛". The canvas and fabric were cut 5" x 14" for the top and bottom border design strips and 5" x 19" for each side border design strip. Begin stitching in the center of each border strip. For both top and bottom border design strips, stitch 5 motifs, ending with half of the lattice and a complete pinwheel at each end. For each side border design strip, stitch 7 motifs, ending in the same manner (see photo).

Corner Motif

FABRICS	DESIGN SIZES
Aida 11	3⅝" x 3⅝"
Aida 14	2¼" x 3⅛"
Aida 18	1¾" x 2⅜"
Hardanger 22	1⅞" x 1⅞"

Border Motif

FABRICS	DESIGN SIZES
Aida 11	2⅞" x 4"
Aida 14	2¼" x 3⅛"
Aida 18	1¾" x 2⅜"
Hardanger 22	1⅜" x 2"

MATERIALS

4 completed cross-stitch corner motifs on rose cotton fabric; matching thread

4 completed cross-stitch borders on lavender cotton fabric; matching thread

1 yard of tan/navy pindot fabric for backing and cats; matching thread

1 yard of navy/gray stripe fabric for border

⅝ yard of white cotton fabric for center section

Scraps of beige print, gray print, brown, and pink fabrics for cats

1 yard (45"-wide) thin cotton batting

3¼ yards (¼") cording

Gold, dark gray, beige, burgundy, and rose embroidery floss for detail on cats

8 assorted flat buttons

White quilting thread

Tracing paper

Water-soluble pen

Frosted vinyl or lightweight cardboard

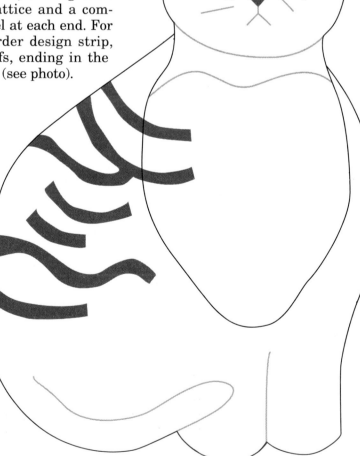

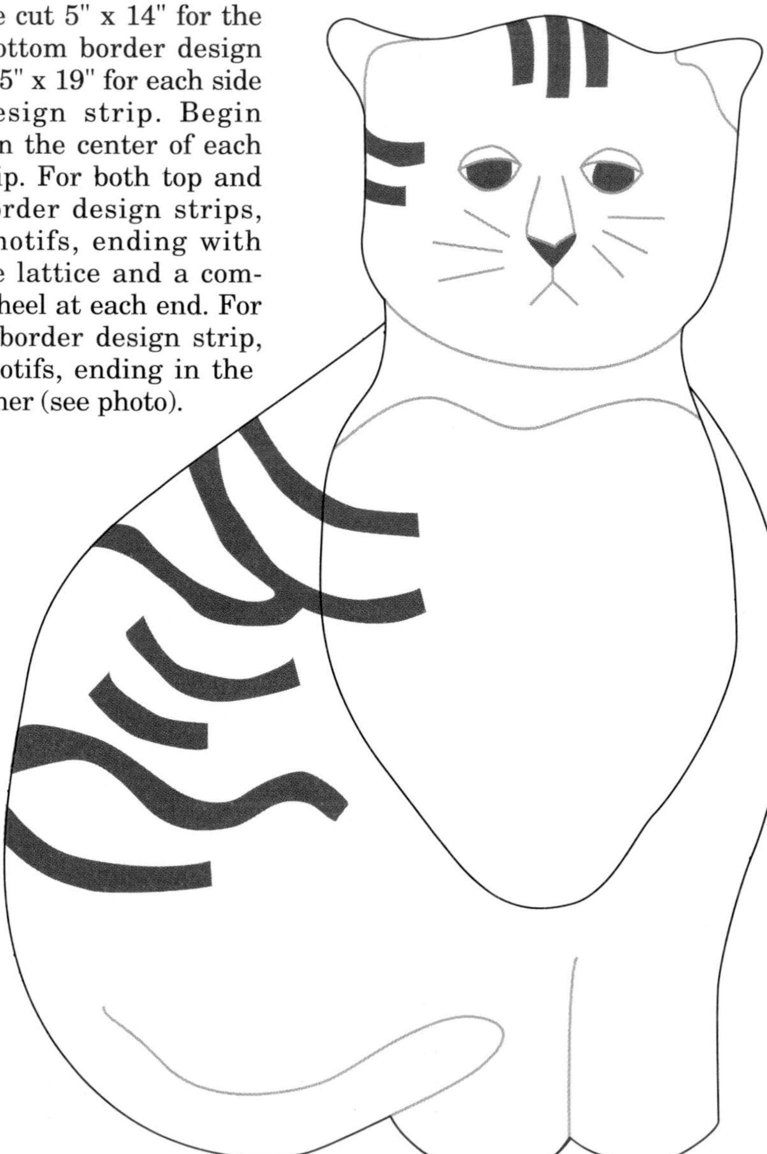

■ *Outline Stitch*

■ *Satin Stitch*

Anchor		DMC	(used for sample)
Step 1: Cross-stitch (2 strands)			
886	-	3047	Yellow Beige-lt.
887	O	3046	Yellow Beige-med.
894	■	223	Shell Pink-med.
846	X	3051	Green Gray-dk.
378	·	841	Beige Brown-lt.
399	X	451	Shell Gray-dk.

DIRECTIONS
All seam allowances are ¼".

1. With designs centered, trim corner motifs to 4½" x 4½", top and bottom border design strips to 4½" x 13½", and side border design strips to 4½" x 18½". From tan/navy pindot fabric, cut 1 (26½" x 31") piece for backing. From navy/gray stripe fabric, cut 2 (2½" x 24½") strips for top and bottom outer borders and 2 (2½" x 29") strips for side outer borders. From white fabric, cut 1 (13¾" x 18½") piece for center section.

2. Using tracing paper, transfer cat face/chest pattern, following gray area of pattern only. Using this pattern, cut 1 pink face/chest and 3 tan/navy pindot face/chest pieces, adding ¼" seam allowances. Using tracing paper, transfer whole cat pattern and cut 1 each from tan/navy pindot, beige print, gray print, and brown fabrics, adding ¼" seam allowances.

Using water-soluble pen, transfer all pattern markings to fabric.

3. To attach cross-stitched borders, with right sides facing and raw edges aligned, stitch 1 side border design strip to each long edge of white center piece. With right sides facing and raw edges aligned, stitch 1 corner motif to each short edge of top and bottom border design strips. With right sides facing and raw edges aligned, stitch top and bottom border design strips to center section (see Diagram A).

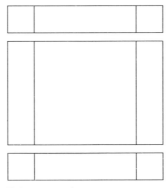

Diagram A

4. To attach outer borders, mark centers of each edge of center section and 1 long edge of each navy/gray stripe outer border strip. With right sides facing, match center of 1 side outer border strip to center of 1 side edge of center section; stitch to within ¼" of corners; backstitch. Repeat with remaining side, top, and bottom outer border strips. Miter corners (see Diagram B).

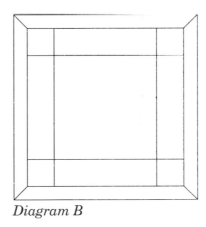

Diagram B

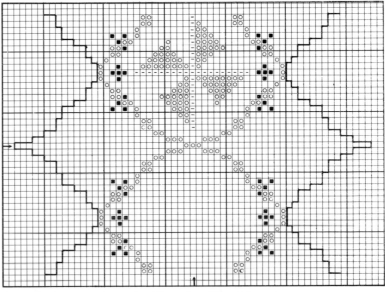

Stitch Count: 40 x 40 (Corner Motif)   **Stitch Count: 31 x 43 (Border Motif)**

Diagram C

5. Fold quilt top into quarters and mark vertical and horizontal centers of white center section, using water-soluble pen. Center 1 whole cat in each quarter. Turn raw edges under ¼" and hand-appliqué cats to center quarter sections. Referring to photo for color placement, position and appliqué face/chest pieces in same manner. Referring to pattern, embroider details on cat bodies and faces, using floss colors as desired.

6. Center and stack backing (right side down); batting; quilt top (right side up). Baste together. To bind edges, beginning in 1 corner, baste cording to outside edge of navy/gray stripe outer border, from corner to corner; cut cording at each corner. Folding fabric toward quilt top, wrap backing over cording once; then fold fabric-covered cording over again to cover raw edge of outer border strip. Slipstitch folded-over edge to right side of quilt top. To turn corner, butt ends of cording together and wrap backing over cording in same manner, squaring corners. Slipstitch. Continue around quilt top. Using 3 strands of contrasting color embroidery floss, stitch a spiral around

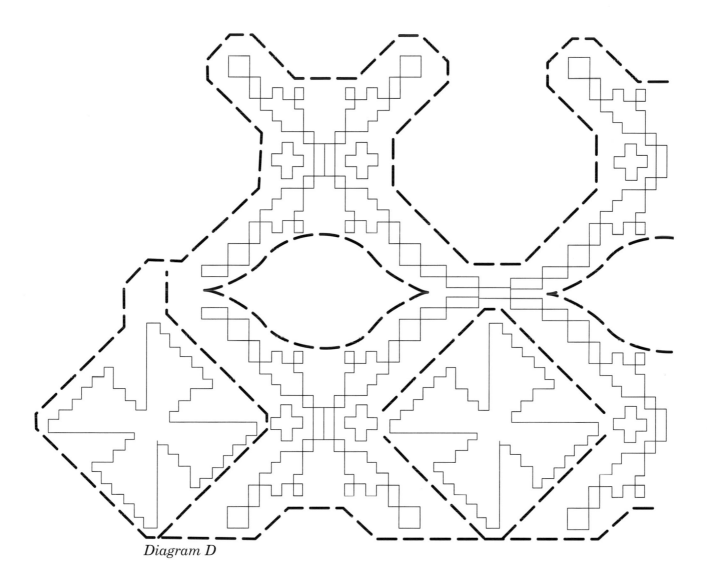

Diagram D

cording, stitching through all layers.

7. Using water-soluble pen, mark a 1" grid on white center section (do not include cats); then mark diagonal quilting lines, 1⅜" apart. Mark quilt lines ¼" inside each seam on navy/gray outer border. Using quilting thread, quilt all marked lines, quilt in-the-ditch along cross-stitched border seams, and outline-quilt around each appliquéd cat. Echo-quilt around each corner motif and outline-quilt around each border design (see Diagrams C and D).

8. Center and stitch buttons on intersecting vertical and horizontal center lines in white section of quilt top (see photo).

JUNE 18–20

Wizard of Oz Convention

*Stuff your night clothes into this
delightful pajama bag and follow the yellow brick
road to fun and fantasy. Each year, young and old alike
are swept away to Zion, Illinois, for a whirlwind
of activities in the Land of Oz. What they discover is
that courage, heart, and brains
abound in us all.*

Pajama Bag

SAMPLE
Stitched on cracked wheat
Murano 30 over 2 threads,
finished design size is 6½" x
4¾". Fabric was cut 15" x 10".

FABRICS	DESIGN SIZES
Aida 11	8⅞" x 6½"
Aida 14	7" x 5⅛"
Aida 18	5⅛" x 4"
Hardanger 22	4½" x 3¼"

MATERIALS
Completed cross-stitch on
   cracked wheat Murano 30
¼ yard (45"-wide) light blue
   chintz; matching thread
½ yard (45"-wide) dusty blue
   chintz

½ yard (45"-wide) gold chintz;
   matching thread
1 (14" x 14") piece of polyester
   batting
3½ yards (¼") cording
2 yards (⅜"-wide) light blue
   satin ribbon, cut in half
2 yards (⅜"-wide) dusty blue
   satin ribbon, cut in half
2 yards (¼"-wide) light blue
   satin ribbon, cut in half
2 yards (¼"-wide) dusty blue
   satin ribbon, cut in half
4 (⅝") lion buttons
Frosted vinyl or lightweight
   cardboard
Dressmaker's pen

DIRECTIONS

The patterns include ¼" seam allowances.

1. With design centered, trim Murano to 14" x 6½". Make template patterns.

2. From light blue chintz, cut 1 (14" x 22½") piece for back, 1 (4" x 14") strip, 10 triangles using Template A, and 2 squares using Template B.

3. From dusty blue chintz, cut 1 (14" x 12") piece for back flap, 1 (14" x 14") piece for lining, 1 (2½" x 14") strip, 14 triangles using Template A, and 4 squares using Template B.

4. From gold chintz, cut 3 (1" x 14") strips, 6 (1" x 3½") pieces, and 5 (1" x 2¼") pieces. From remaining gold chintz, cut 1"-wide bias strips, piecing as needed to equal 3½ yards. Make 1½ yards of corded piping.

5. To make corded tubing for handle and ties: With right sides facing, raw edges aligned, and matching long edges, fold remaining 2 yards of bias strip in half and stitch, leaving ends open for turning. Trim seam allowance to ⅛"; turn right side out. Using bodkin, thread remaining cording through casing. Cut length of corded tubing in half. Fold ends in ⅛" and slipstitch closed. Set aside.

6. To assemble pieced section, with right sides facing and raw edges aligned, join diagonal edges of 1 light blue A and 1 dusty blue A. Repeat to make 6 squares. With right sides facing and raw edges aligned, stitch 1 (1" x 2¼") gold piece to 1 dusty blue edge of 3 squares; then stitch 1 (1" x 2¼") gold piece to 1

light blue edge of 2 of remaining squares. Join all squares in strip, arranging colors as desired. Refering to Diagram and photo, with right sides facing and raw edges aligned, stitch pieces together to complete front of bag. Sew buttons on light blue strip (see Diagram for placement).

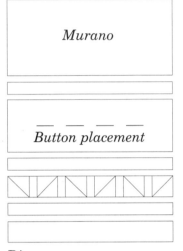

Diagram

7. Stack dusty blue lining piece (right side down); batting; design front (right side up). Baste together. With right sides facing and raw edges aligned, stitch corded piping to right side of bag front, stitching through all layers and rounding corners slightly. Trim batting from seam allowance.

8. To make envelope back: With wrong sides facing and matching long edges, fold dusty blue 14" x 12" back flap piece in half lengthwise. Place on right side of design front, matching raw edges at top and sides. With wrong sides facing and matching short edges, fold light blue 14" x 22½" back piece in half lengthwise. Place on right side of design front, matching raw edges at sides and bottom

and overlapping dusty blue back flap piece. Stitch back flap piece and back piece to design piece along stitching line of corded piping. Turn.

9. To make 2 light blue/gold stuffed squares and 4 dusty blue/gold stuffed squares for trim: With right sides facing and raw edges aligned, join diagonal edges of 2 As of the same shade of blue to each long edge of 1 (1" x 3½") gold piece. Repeat with remaining As. With right sides facing and raw edges aligned, stitch together 1 pieced front to 1 B cut from matching shade of blue, leaving an opening. Turn and stuff. Slipstitch opening closed. Repeat with remaining pieced fronts and Bs to complete 6 stuffed squares.

10. From corded tubing pieces that were set aside for handle and ties, fold 1 piece into a 10½" deep loop with ends of corded tubing in uneven lengths. With longer free end, make a knot around loop, leaving a 3½" loop above knot and a 3" single length of corded tubing hanging below, along with shorter free end. Tack knot to 1 top corner of bag. Repeat with remaining corded tubing, first threading length through large loop of other piece to form handle. Tack 1 stuffed square to each free end of corded tubing and to each short loop (see photo).

11. Divide ribbon halves equally into 2 groups of 4 pieces each; knot ends of each length. Handling each group of ribbon as 1, make a bow and tack 1 to each corded tubing knot.

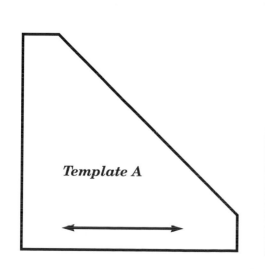

Template A

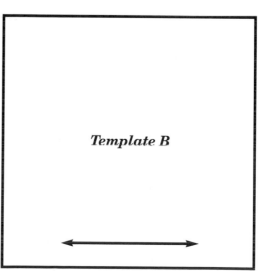

Template B

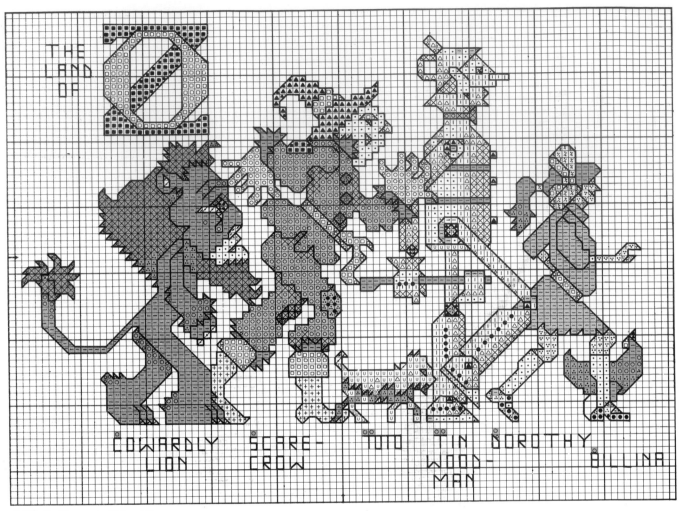

Stitch Count: 98 x 71

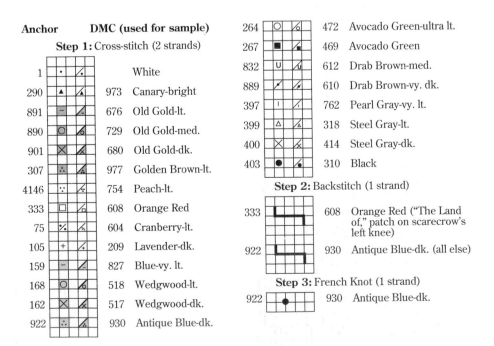

Anchor			DMC	(used for sample)
			Step 1:	Cross-stitch (2 strands)
1	·	⁄		White
290	▲	⁄	973	Canary-bright
891	–	⁄	676	Old Gold-lt.
890	◯	⁄	729	Old Gold-med.
901	✕	⁄	680	Old Gold-dk.
307	∴	⁄	977	Golden Brown-lt.
4146	∷	⁄	754	Peach-lt.
333	☐	⁄	608	Orange Red
75	⁒	⁄	604	Cranberry-lt.
105	+	⁄	209	Lavender-dk.
159	–	⁄	827	Blue-vy. lt.
168	◯	⁄	518	Wedgwood-lt.
162	✕	⁄	517	Wedgwood-dk.
922	∴	⁄	930	Antique Blue-dk.

Anchor			DMC	
264	◯	⁄	472	Avocado Green-ultra lt.
267	■	⁄	469	Avocado Green
832	U	⁄	612	Drab Brown-med.
889	⁄	⁄	610	Drab Brown-vy. dk.
397	I	⁄	762	Pearl Gray-vy. lt.
399	△	⁄	318	Steel Gray-lt.
400	✕	⁄	414	Steel Gray-dk.
403	●	⁄	310	Black

Step 2: Backstitch (1 strand)

333		608	Orange Red ("The Land of," patch on scarecrow's left knee)
922		930	Antique Blue-dk. (all else)

Step 3: French Knot (1 strand)

922	●	930	Antique Blue-dk.

80

JUNE 27
Singing on the Mountain

*In Linville, North Carolina, the fourth Sunday
of June is set aside for the sounds of gospel music. Cool
breezes keep spirits high atop Grandfather Mountain,
while singing echoes through the surrounding valleys.*

82

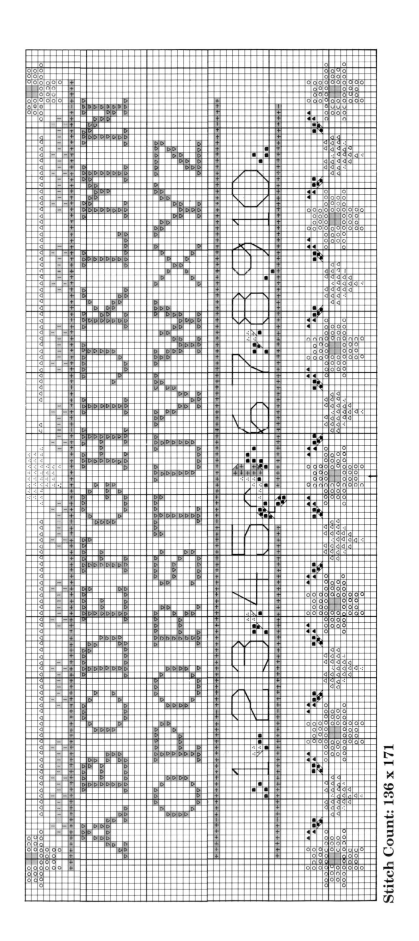

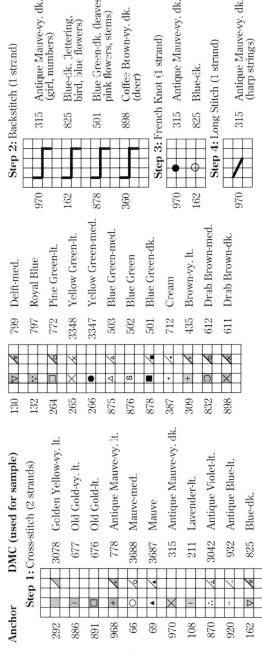

Anchor			DMC (used for sample)
			Step 1: Cross-stitch (2 strands)
292			3078 Golden Yellow-vy. lt.
886		−	677 Old Gold-vy. lt.
891		□	676 Old Gold-lt.
968		+	778 Antique Mauve-vy. lt.
66		○	3688 Mauve-med.
69		▲	3687 Mauve
970		✕	315 Antique Mauve-vy. dk.
108		−	211 Lavender-lt.
870		∴	3042 Antique Violet-lt.
920		−	932 Antique Blue-lt.
162		▽	825 Blue-dk.

130	▽		799 Delft-med.
132	∴		797 Royal Blue
264	□		772 Pine Green-lt.
265	✕		3348 Yellow Green-lt.
266	●		3347 Yellow Green-med.
875	△		503 Blue Green-lt.
876	s		502 Blue Green
878	■		501 Blue Green-dk.
387	·		712 Cream
309	+		435 Brown-vy. lt.
832	○		612 Drab Brown-med.
898	✕		611 Drab Brown-dk.

Step 2: Backstitch (1 strand)

970		315	Antique Mauve-vy. dk. (girl, numbers)
162		825	Blue-dk. (lettering, bird, blue flowers)
878		501	Blue Green-dk. (leaves, pink flowers, stems)
360		898	Coffee Brown-vy. dk. (deer)

Step 3: French Knot (1 strand)

| ● | 970 | | 315 | Antique Mauve-vy. dk. |
| ⊕ | 162 | | 825 | Blue-dk. |

Step 4: Long Stitch (1 strand)

| ╱ | 970 | | 315 | Antique Mauve-vy. dk. (harp strings) |

Sweet Sounds of Summer

SAMPLE

Stitched on sand Dublin Linen 25 over 2 threads, the finished design size is 10⅞" x 13⅝". The fabric was cut 17" x 20".

FABRICS	DESIGN SIZES
Aida 11	12⅜" x 15½"
Aida 14	9¾" x 12¼"
Aida 18	7½" x 9½"
Hardanger 22	6⅛" x 7¾"

JULY 11
Old Crafts Day

Woodworking and needlework are two of the time-honored crafts demonstrated at Old Crafts Day each July in Fond du Lac, Wisconsin. To commemorate these skills, we have embellished a purchased box base to make this old-fashioned sewing accessory.

Old-fashioned Sewing Box

SAMPLE
Stitched on Linaida 14 over 1 thread, the finished design size is 2¼" x 2⅝" for each. The fabric was cut 6" x 6" for each. Stitch 2. See Suppliers for material.

MATERIALS
2 completed cross-stitch designs on Linaida 14; matching thread
½ yard (⅛") purchased pink satin cording, cut in half
Stuffing
Tracing paper
Scrap of ¾"-thick wood
Scrap of ⅛"-thick pressboard
Band saw or jigsaw
7½" piece of ¼" dowel
1" piece of ⅜" dowel
Sandpaper
1 (6" x 6" x 3") purchased wooden box with drawer
Glue
Drill with ¼", ⅜" bits
Wood file
Wood stain or paint in desired color
Paintbrush
Dressmaker's pen
Sewing scissors, spools of thread, and other notions

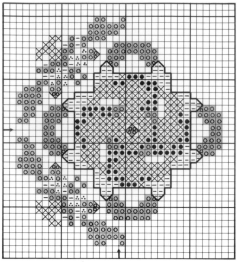

Stitch Count: 32 x 36

Anchor			DMC (used for sample)	
Step 1: Cross-stitch (2 strands)				
8	-	⁄	761	Salmon-lt.
10	✕		3712	Salmon-med.
11	●		3328	Salmon-dk.
969	∴		316	Antique Mauve-med.
160	◐	⁄	813	Blue-lt.
860	◐	⁄	3053	Green Gray
Step 2: Backstitch (1 strand)				
11			3328	Salmon-dk.

DIRECTIONS

1. Transfer bird and wing pattern to tracing paper and cut out. Mark bird pattern on wood and cut 1, using saw. Trace wing pattern on pressboard and cut 2. Set aside.

2. Cut ¼" dowel into 6 (1¼"-long) pieces. Sand ¼" and ⅜" dowels. For spool holders, using ¼" bit, drill 3 (¼"-deep) holes at 1¾" intervals, ¼" from each left and right edge and ¾" from front and back edges of box top (see Diagram). Using ⅜" bit, drill 1 (½"-deep) hole 2" from bird's tail (see pattern). Glue dowels in place.

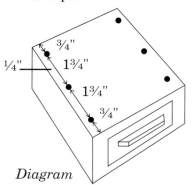

Diagram

3. Mark placement on top and bottom of bird head for scissors opening. Using ¼" bit,

drill 4 holes side by side all the way through bird's head. File through holes, making a 1" x ⅜" opening. Sand bird and box smooth. Stain or paint as desired. Mark wing placement on bird. Center and glue bird to box top (see photo).

4. Place wing pattern on wrong side of each design piece, with blue stitching centered in widest end of each wing; trace with a dressmaker's pen. Trim design pieces 1" outside marked lines. Run a gathering thread ¼" from each raw edge.

5. Glue a moderate amount of stuffing to 1 side of 1 pressboard wing. Center wrong side of design piece over stuffing. Pull thread to gather fabric to wrong side of pressboard wing; secure thread. With wide end of wing facing bird's breast, glue wing to bird. Repeat for other wing. Glue a 9" length of satin cording around each wing (see photo).

6. Place scissors through opening in head. Add other notions as desired.

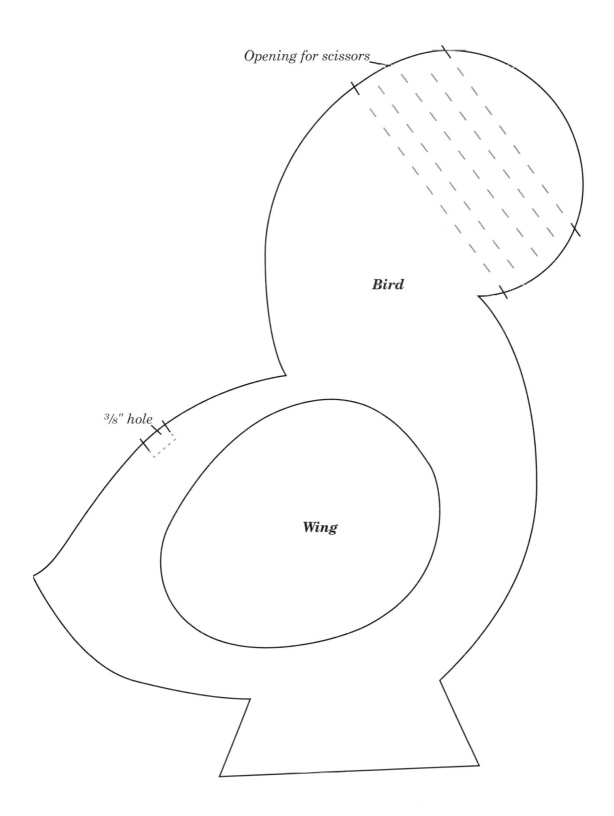

Opening for scissors

Bird

³/₈″ hole

Wing

AUGUST 12
Baby Parade

"Babies are bits of stardust blown from the hand of God," according to one philosopher. In Ocean City, New Jersey, the townspeople honor these special little citizens with their very own annual parade. For the babies in your world, here is a parade of five storybook animal blocks to keep little ones happy for hours.

Storybook Animals

SAMPLE for Rabbit and Duck

Stitched on carnation Pastel Linen 28 over 2 threads, the finished design size for each is 2¾" x 2⅞". The fabric was cut 9" x 9" for each.

SAMPLE for Lamb

Stitched on pistachio Pastel Linen 28 over 2 threads, the finished design size is 2¾" x 2⅞". The fabric was cut 9" x 9".

SAMPLE for Cat

Stitched on periwinkle Pastel Linen 28 over 2 threads, the finished design size is 2¾" x 2⅞". The fabric was cut 9" x 9".

SAMPLE for Dog

Stitched on daffodil Pastel Linen 28 over 2 threads, the finished design size is 2¾" x 2⅞". The fabric was cut 9" x 9".

FABRICS	DESIGN SIZES
Aida 11	3½" x 3¾"
Aida 14	2¾" x 2⅞"
Aida 18	2⅛" x 2¼"
Hardanger 22	1¾" x 1⅞"

MATERIALS (for 5 blocks)

5 completed cross-stitch designs on Pastel Linen 28 (see Sample information)
⅛ yard each of unstitched carnation, pistachio, periwinkle, and daffodil Pastel Linen 28
1½ yards of polyester batting
Embroidery floss in coordinating colors (from design pieces)
1 (16" x 16" x 2") foam pillow form
White thread
Glue

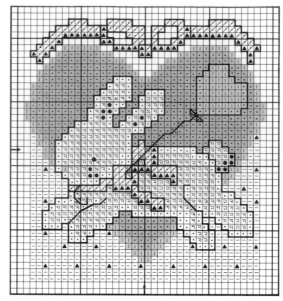

Stitch Count: 38 x 41 (Rabbit)

DIRECTIONS

All seam allowances are ¼".

1. With design centered, trim each design piece to 5" x 5". Cut 7 (5" x 5") pieces each from 2 colors of unstitched linen, 6 from another color, and 5 from remaining color.

2. From pillow form, cut 10 (4" x 4" x 2") pieces. Set remaining foam aside for another use. Stack and glue foam pieces together in pairs, forming blocks. From batting, cut 5 (4" x 16") strips and 10 (4" x 4") pieces. To cover each foam block, wrap 1 batting strip around block; slipstitch ends together. Cover each remaining side with 1 (4" x 4") batting piece; slipstitch edges to batting strip.

3. To complete 1 block, select 1 design piece and 5 unstitched pieces, alternating colors as desired. With right sides facing and raw edges aligned, stitch 1 edge of 1 unstitched piece to 1 side edge of design piece. Stitch

an additional plain piece to each remaining side of these squares to make a strip of 4 (see Diagram). With right sides facing and raw edges aligned, stitch ends together to make a tube.

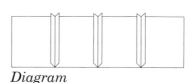

Diagram

4. For top of block, with right sides facing and raw edges aligned, place fifth unstitched piece inside tube, matching corners. Stitch, beginning in 1 corner and stitching to, but not through, next side seam; backstitch. Repeat for each remaining edge to complete top.

5. With right sides facing and raw edges aligned, stitch 1 edge *only* of remaining unstitched piece to 1 edge of block bottom in same manner.

6. Turn right side out; insert foam block. Fold partially attached square over opening.

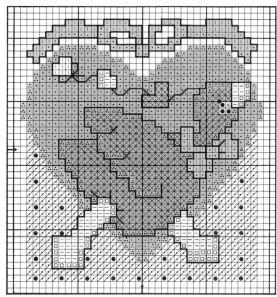

Stitch Count: 38 x 41 (Duck)

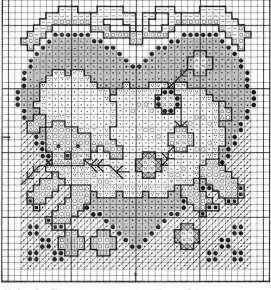

Stitch Count: 38 x 41 (Lamb)

Turn under ¼" seam allowance, matching corners to side seams, and slipstitch remaining sides closed. Using 2 strands of 1 coordinating floss, feather-stitch over each seam, alternating colors for each block. Repeat to make remaining blocks.

Rabbit Block

Anchor		DMC	(used for sample)

Step 1: Cross-stitch (2 strands)

1			White
300	−	745	Yellow-lt. pale
48	·	818	Baby Pink
25	⁄.	3326	Rose-lt.
27	●	899	Rose-med.
108	i	211	Lavender-lt.
104	·	210	Lavender-med.
208	╱	563	Jade-lt.
210	▲	562	Jade-med.
397	·	762	Pearl Gray-vy. lt.

Step 2: Backstitch (1 strand)

400		317	Pewter Gray

Step 3: French Knot (1 strand)

400	●	317	Pewter Gray

Duck Block

Anchor		DMC	(used for sample)

Step 1: Cross-stitch (2 strands)

300	−	745	Yellow-lt. pale
301	□	744	Yellow-pale
48	·	818	Baby Pink
25	⁄.	3326	Rose-lt.
27	●	899	Rose-med.
108	i	211	Lavender-lt.
104	·	210	Lavender-med.
128	∴	800	Delft-pale
130	✕	809	Delft
208	╱	563	Jade-lt.
376	✕	842	Beige Brown-vy. lt.
378	∴	841	Beige Brown-lt.

Step 2: Backstitch (1 strand)

400		317	Pewter Gray

Step 3: French Knot (1 strand)

400	●	317	Pewter Gray

Lamb Block

Anchor		DMC	(used for sample)

Step 1: Cross-stitch (2 strands)

300	−	745	Yellow-lt. pale
301	□	744	Yellow-pale
48	·	818	Baby Pink
25	⁄.	3326	Rose-lt.
27	●	899	Rose-med.
108	i	211	Lavender-lt.
104	·	210	Lavender-med.
130	✕	809	Delft
208	╱	563	Jade-lt.
397	·	762	Pearl Gray-vy. lt.
398	○	415	Pearl Gray
399	∴	318	Steel Gray-lt.
400	△	414	Steel Gray-dk.
401	■	317	Pewter Gray

Step 2: Backstitch (1 strand)

210		562	Jade-med. (2 strands) (flower stems)
401		317	Pewter Gray (all else)

Step 3: French Knot (1 strand)

401	●	317	Pewter Gray

Cat Block

Anchor   DMC (used for sample)

Step 1: Cross-stitch (2 strands)

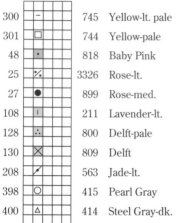

Anchor		DMC	
300	–	745	Yellow-lt. pale
301	□	744	Yellow-pale
48	·	818	Baby Pink
25	⁒	3326	Rose-lt.
27	●	899	Rose-med.
108	I	211	Lavender-lt.
128	∴	800	Delft-pale
130	⊠	809	Delft
208	╱	563	Jade-lt.
398	○	415	Pearl Gray
400	△	414	Steel Gray-dk.

Step 2: Backstitch (1 strand)

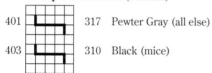

401		317	Pewter Gray (all else)
403		310	Black (mice)

Step 3: French Knot (1 strand)

401	●	317	Pewter Gray (balloons and cat)
403	■	310	Black (mice)

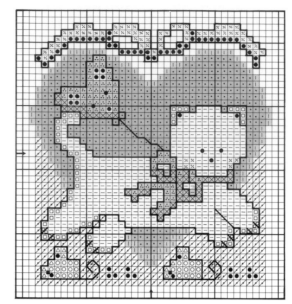

Stitch Count: 38 x 41 (Cat)

Dog Block

Anchor   DMC (used for sample)

Step 1: Cross-stitch (2 strands)

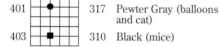

Anchor		DMC	
386	I	746	Off White
48	·	818	Baby Pink
25	⁒	3326	Rose-lt.
27	●	899	Rose-med.
108	I	211	Lavender-lt.
128	∴	800	Delft-pale
130	⊠	809	Delft
208	╱	563	Jade-lt.
210	▲	562	Jade-med.
376	⊠	842	Beige Brown-vy. lt.
378	∴	841	Beige Brown-lt.

Step 2: Backstitch (1 strand)

400		317	Pewter Gray

Step 3: French Knot (1 strand)

400	●	317	Pewter Gray

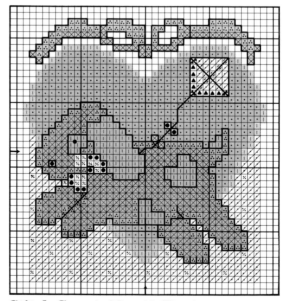

Stitch Count: 38 x 41 (Dog)

Jane Addams' Birthday

In 1889, Jane Addams founded Hull House, one of the first social settlements in North America. Her work for social reform and workmen's compensation earned her the Nobel Peace Prize in 1931. We honor Jane's accomplishments with this lovely doll.

Sachet Doll

SAMPLE
Stitched on periwinkle Pastel Linen 28 over 2 threads, the finished design size is 6¾" x 7¾" for each skirt piece. See Step 1 of Directions before cutting fabric. See Suppliers for porcelain doll kit.

MATERIALS
¼ yard of unstitched periwinkle Pastel Linen 28; matching thread
½ yard (¼"-wide) dusty rose satin ribbon
¼ yard (¼"-wide) white lace
Stuffing
1 (¼") blue cameo shank button
1 Abigail porcelain doll kit (see Suppliers)
2 cups of uncooked rice
2 cups of potpourri
10" (½"-wide) dowel
10" florist's wire
Tracing paper
Dressmaker's pen

DIRECTIONS

The patterns include ¼" seam allowances.

1. Make patterns for bodice, skirt, and base. With dressmaker's pen, trace 2 skirt patterns on linen and cut out. Work cross-stitch design, beginning in center of each skirt piece. Stitch to fill area. Cut 2 bodice pieces and 1 base from remaining unstitched linen.

2. For dress front, with right sides facing and raw edges aligned, stitch 1 bodice to 1 skirt piece at waist. Repeat for back. With right sides facing and raw edges aligned, stitch dress front to back along sides and underarms, matching designs at seams. Clip underarm seam allowances. With right sides facing and raw edges aligned, stitch base to bottom of skirt. Stitch 1 shoulder seam from cuff to neck edge. Stitch second shoulder seam from cuff to 1" from neck edge, leaving an opening. Do not turn.

3. Cut lace into 3 (3") pieces; set 1 piece aside for neck. Run a gathering thread along straight edge of 1 lace piece and pull to gather to fit 1 cuff. With straight edges aligned, baste to right side of cuff. Run a second gathering thread through both layers. Do not cut thread. With dress still wrong side out, insert porcelain arm and gather cuff tightly ¼" from groove at top of arm. Secure thread. Repeat for remaining arm. Turn dress. Sew cameo button to top center front of dress (see photo).

4. Fill bottom half of skirt with rice and potpourri. Score dowel 2" from top and insert. Stuff dress firmly so dowel will stand straight in center of dress. Wrap center of florist's wire tightly around score line and then wrap wire tails around grooves in porcelain arms (see Diagram). Stuff sleeves firmly.

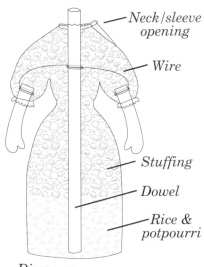

Neck/sleeve opening

Wire

Stuffing

Dowel

Rice & potpourri

Diagram

5. Run a gathering thread along straight edge of remaining lace piece; gather to fit neck. Baste to right side of neck. Run a second gathering thread through both layers. Do not cut thread. Place doll head on top of dowel. Pull thread to gather lace tightly around neck. Secure thread. Stuff bodice through opening in sleeve. Slipstitch opening closed.

6. Cut 1 (3½") piece of ribbon. Fold ribbon in half lengthwise, matching long edges. Wrap around neck and tack ends to back at neck. Wrap remaining ribbon twice around waist; tack ends to back of waist.

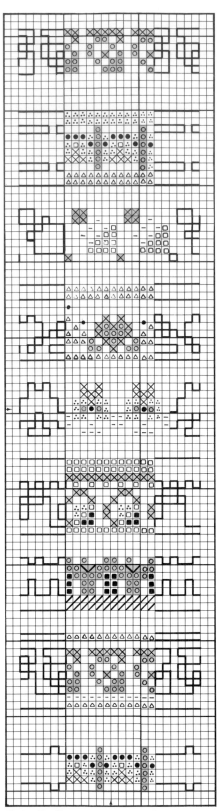

Stitch Count: 112 x 167

94

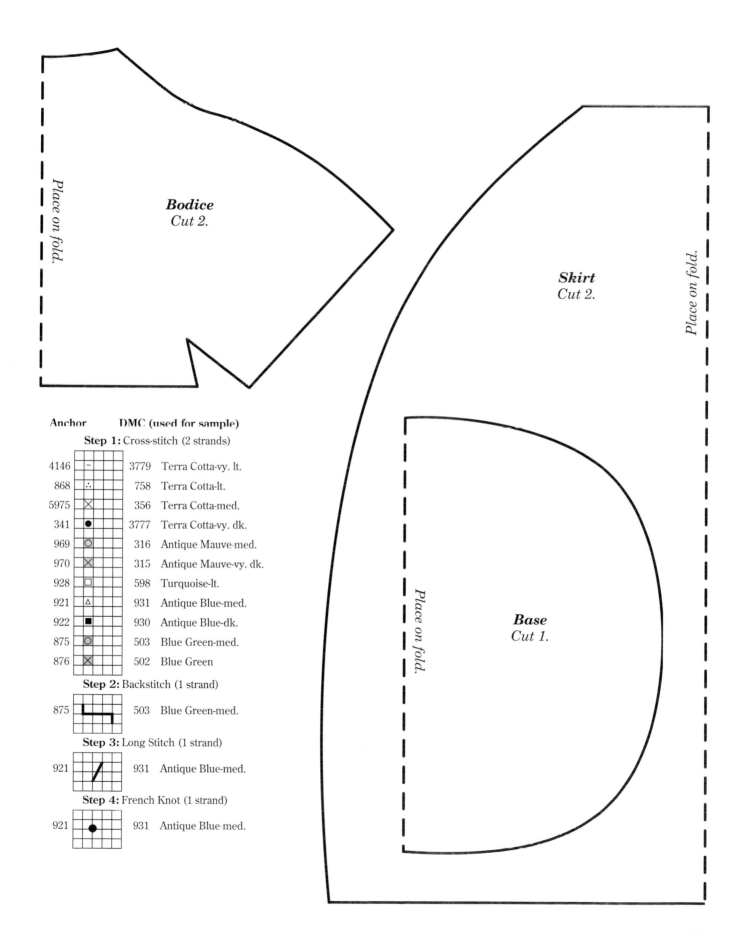

Bodice
Cut 2.

Place on fold.

Skirt
Cut 2.

Place on fold.

Base
Cut 1.

Place on fold.

Anchor   DMC (used for sample)

Step 1: Cross-stitch (2 strands)

Anchor		DMC	
4146	–	3779	Terra Cotta-vy. lt.
868	∴	758	Terra Cotta-lt.
5975	✕	356	Terra Cotta-med.
341	●	3777	Terra Cotta-vy. dk.
969	◯	316	Antique Mauve-med.
970	✕	315	Antique Mauve-vy. dk.
928	□	598	Turquoise-lt.
921	△	931	Antique Blue-med.
922	■	930	Antique Blue-dk.
875	◯	503	Blue Green-med.
876	✕	502	Blue Green

Step 2: Backstitch (1 strand)

| 875 | | 503 | Blue Green-med. |

Step 3: Long Stitch (1 strand)

| 921 | ╱ | 931 | Antique Blue-med. |

Step 4: French Knot (1 strand)

| 921 | ● | 931 | Antique Blue-med. |

National Good Neighbor Day

Welcome a new family into your neighborhood or show a family you've known for years how much you appreciate their friendship with this colorful cross-stitched piece. As this scene shows, good neighbors need not only be the families next door to you but across the street or down the block!

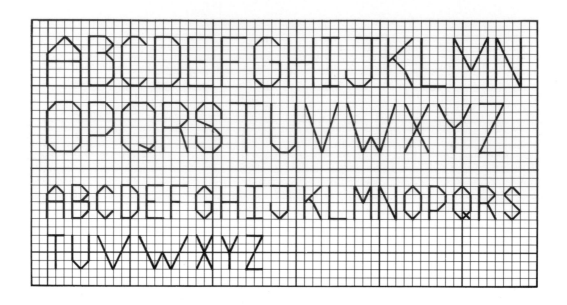

Welcome, Neighbor

SAMPLE
Stitched on Linaida 14 over 1 thread, the finished design size is 5½" x 5½". The fabric was cut 12" x 12". See Suppliers for material.

FABRICS | **DESIGN SIZES**
Aida 11 | 6⅞" x 6⅞"
Aida 14 | 5½" x 5½"
Aida 18 | 4¼" x 4¼"
Hardanger 22 | 3½" x 3½"

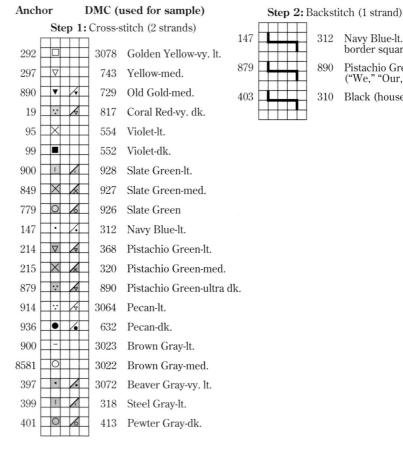

Anchor		DMC (used for sample)	
Step 1: Cross-stitch (2 strands)			
292		3078	Golden Yellow-vy. lt.
297		743	Yellow-med.
890		729	Old Gold-med.
19		817	Coral Red-vy. dk.
95		554	Violet-lt.
99		552	Violet-dk.
900		928	Slate Green-lt.
849		927	Slate Green-med.
779		926	Slate Green
147		312	Navy Blue-lt.
214		368	Pistachio Green-lt.
215		320	Pistachio Green-med.
879		890	Pistachio Green-ultra dk.
914		3064	Pecan-lt.
936		632	Pecan-dk.
900		3023	Brown Gray-lt.
8581		3022	Brown Gray-med.
397		3072	Beaver Gray-vy. lt.
399		318	Steel Gray-lt.
401		413	Pewter Gray-dk.

Step 2: Backstitch (1 strand)

147		312	Navy Blue-lt. (names, border squares)
879		890	Pistachio Green-ultra dk. ("We," "Our," "Street")
403		310	Black (houses, trees)

Stitch Count: 76 x 76

OCTOBER
Wine Festival Month

*Wine, a drink hailed
by ancients and
moderns, kings and
commoners alike, is the
reason for many autumn
festivals and celebrations
all across the country.
In addition to wine
tasting, some of
these events include
food booths and tributes
to Bacchus, the Greek god
of wine. Here, the revered
drink is honored in the
form of a clock, a rich
and elegant addition
to any room.*

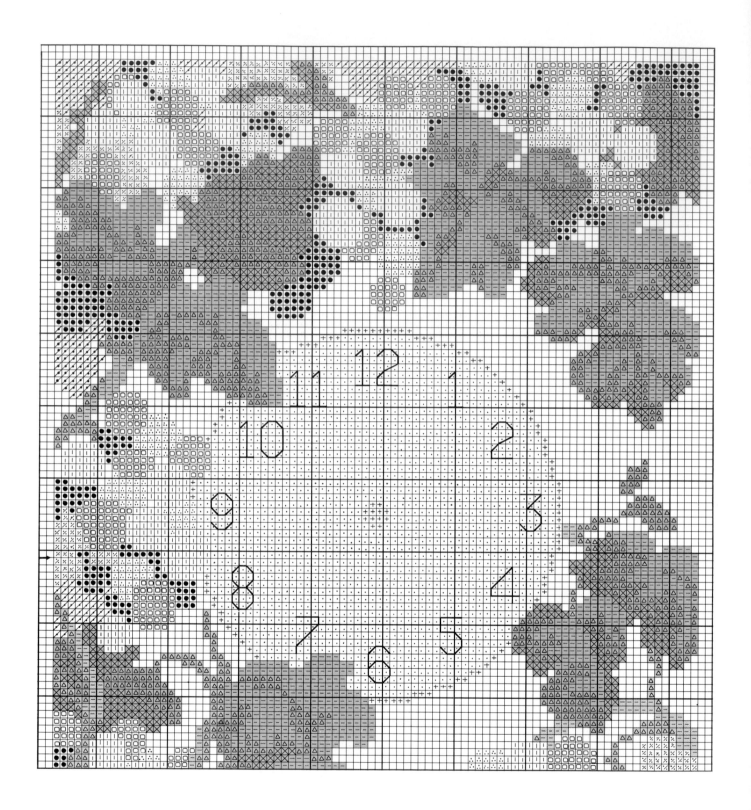

102

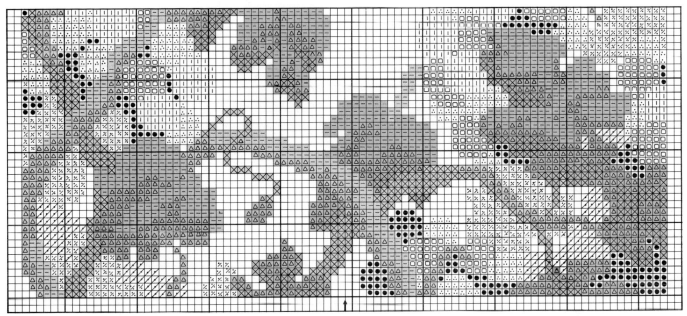

Stitch Count: 90 x 138

Time for Wine

SAMPLE

Stitched on natural Linen 28 over 2 threads, the finished design size is 6⅜" x 9⅞". The fabric was cut 13" x 16". Mount needlework on ⅛"-thick, acid-free mounting board. Install clock movement and hands according to manufacturer's instructions. Frame with molding that is at least 1⅞" deep.

FABRICS	DESIGN SIZES
Aida 11	8⅛" x 12½"
Aida 14	6⅜" x 9⅞"
Aida 18	5" x 7⅝"
Hardanger 22	4⅛" x 6¼"

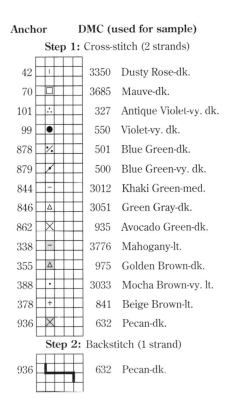

Anchor		DMC (used for sample)	
		Step 1: Cross-stitch (2 strands)	
42	I	3350	Dusty Rose-dk.
70	□	3685	Mauve-dk.
101	∴	327	Antique Violet-vy. dk.
99	●	550	Violet-vy. dk.
878	╱	501	Blue Green-dk.
879	╱	500	Blue Green-vy. dk.
844	−	3012	Khaki Green-med.
846	△	3051	Green Gray-dk.
862	✕	935	Avocado Green-dk.
338	−	3776	Mahogany-lt.
355	△	975	Golden Brown-dk.
388	·	3033	Mocha Brown-vy. lt.
378	+	841	Beige Brown-lt.
936	✕	632	Pecan-dk.
		Step 2: Backstitch (1 strand)	
936		632	Pecan-dk.

OCTOBER 3-9
National Newspaper Week

*Noah Webster
founded America's first
daily newspaper,
The American Minerva,
in 1793. For ten years,
he edited the strongly
Federalist paper himself.
This sampler,
stitched in early-American
blues and browns, honors
the 200th anniversary of
one of our country's
strongest sources of
information,
the daily paper.*

104

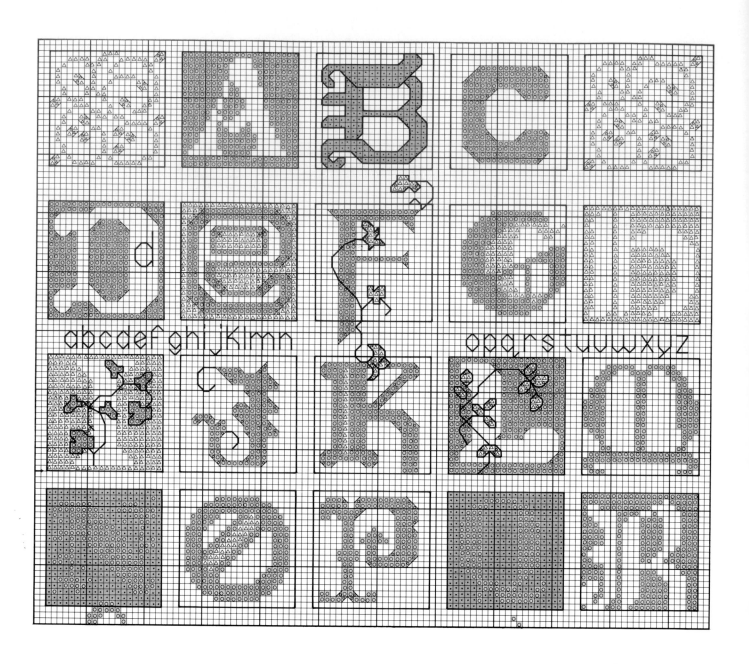

abcdefghijklmn   opqrstuvwxyz

Stitch Count: 112 x 144

Newsletters

SAMPLE
Stitched on cream Cork Linen 19 over 2 threads, the finished design size is 11¾" x 15⅛". The fabric was cut 18" x 22". See Suppliers for Overture yarns and material.

FABRICS	DESIGN SIZES
Aida 11	10⅛" x 13⅛"
Aida 14	8" x 10¼"
Aida 18	6¼" x 8"
Hardanger 22	5⅛" x 6½"

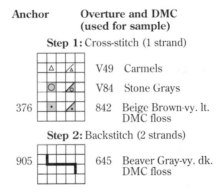

Anchor		Overture and DMC (used for sample)

Step 1: Cross-stitch (1 strand)

		V49	Carmels
		V84	Stone Grays
376		842	Beige Brown-vy. lt. DMC floss

Step 2: Backstitch (2 strands)

905		645	Beaver Gray-vy. dk. DMC floss

National Job Skills Week

*Children love being asked,
"What are you going to be when you grow up?"
And their answers are as varied and delightful
as their young faces. This colorful afghan
presents enough ideas to keep any child's
imagination busy with possibilities.*

When I Grow Up

SAMPLE

Stitched on Vanessa-Ann Afghan Weave 18 over 2 threads. Fabric was cut 45" x 54" (width measurement includes 7 whole blocks and ½ block on each side and length measurement includes 8 whole blocks and ½ on each end). Stitching area of each woven block is 88 x 88 threads. To personalize your design, transfer child's name and birth announcement to graph paper. Mark graph centers and begin stitching in center of spaces indicated (see Diagram). See Suppliers for afghan material.

MATERIALS

Completed cross-stitch on
   Vanessa-Ann Afghan
   Weave 18
⅓ yard (45"-wide) dark green
   fabric; matching thread

DIRECTIONS

1. Cut slightly rounded corners on design piece. Cut 2½"-wide bias strips from dark green fabric, piecing as needed to make 6 yards.

2. To bind edges, with right sides facing and raw edges aligned, pin strip along edges of design piece, allowing extra fullness at corners. Stitch with ⅝" seam, easing in fabric at corners.

3. Fold under ⅝" on remaining raw edge of bias strip; fold to wrong side, binding raw edge of afghan. Slipstitch in place, covering stitching line; easing fabric at corners. Slipstitch corner folds in place.

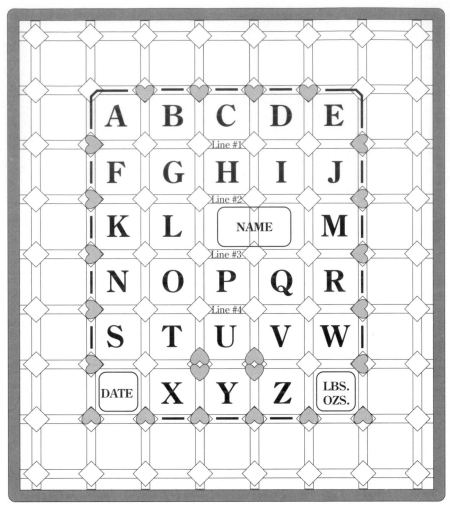

Diagram

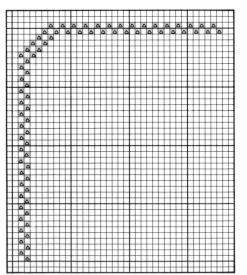

Stitch Count: 35 x 41 (Corner Section)
Stitch Count: 24 x 2 (Short Blue Lines)
Stitch Count: 2 x 36 (Long Blue Lines)

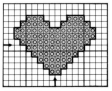

**Stitch Count: 14 x 10
(Single Heart)**

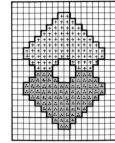

**Stitch Count: 14 x 20
(Double Heart)**

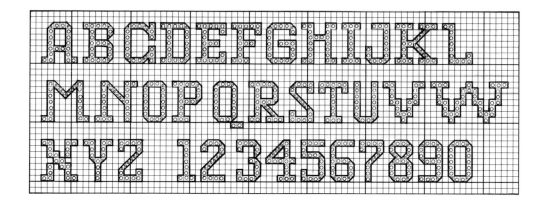

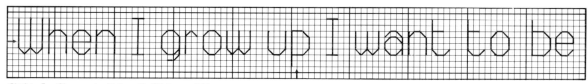

Stitch Count: 94 x 8 (Line #1)

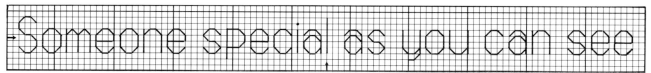

Stitch Count: 104 x 7 (Line #2)

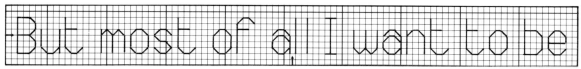

Stitch Count: 93 x 6 (Line #3)

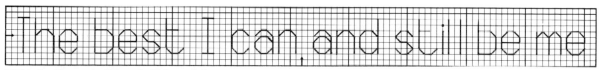

Stitch Count: 96 x 6 (Line #4)

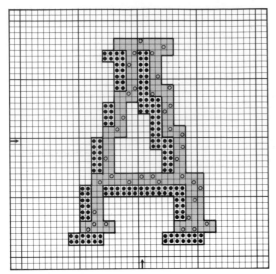

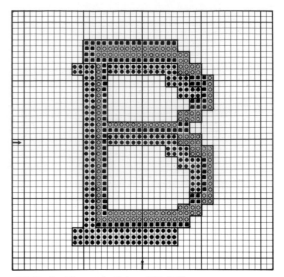

Stitch Count: 25 x 35 (A)   **Stitch Count: 24 x 35 (B)**

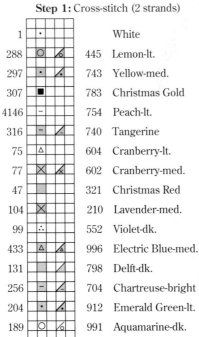

Anchor		DMC (used for sample)	

Step 1: Cross-stitch (2 strands)

1	·			White
288	○	⟋	445	Lemon-lt.
297	·	⟋	743	Yellow-med.
307	■		783	Christmas Gold
4146	–		754	Peach-lt.
316	–	⟋	740	Tangerine
75	△		604	Cranberry-lt.
77	✕	⟋	602	Cranberry-med.
47			321	Christmas Red
104	✕		210	Lavender-med.
99	∴		552	Violet-dk.
433	△	⟋	996	Electric Blue-med.
131		⟋	798	Delft-dk.
256	–	⟋	704	Chartreuse-bright
204	·	⟋	912	Emerald Green-lt.
189	○	⟋	991	Aquamarine-dk.
308	▲		976	Golden Brown-med.
398	☐		415	Pearl Gray
400	✕		414	Steel Gray-dk.
403	●	⟋	310	Black

Step 2: Cross-stitch (2 strands)

	○		
	+		
	∴		

Stitch hearts in corners and borders using colors as desired; see photo.

Step 3: Backstitch (1 strand)

433		996	Electric Blue-med. (white and blue part of "R," pink and blue part of "S")
131		793	Delft-dk. (lettering on "I")
189		991	Aquamarine-dk. (flowers on "F")
398		415	Pearl Gray (pink and gray part of "V")
403		310	Black (all else)

Step 4: French Knot (1 strand)

| 403 | ● | 310 | Black |

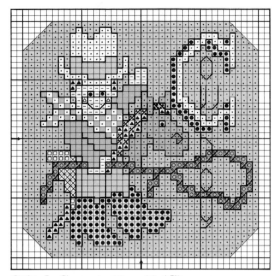

Stitch Count: 40 x 40 (C)

Stitch Count: 40 x 40 (D)

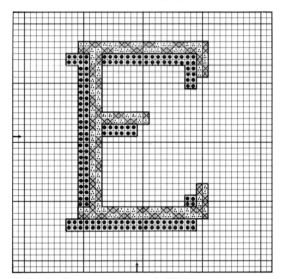

Stitch Count: 24 x 32 (E)

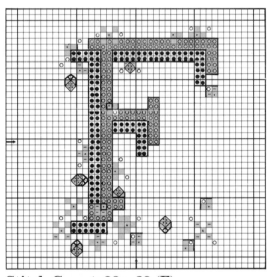

Stitch Count: 28 x 39 (F)

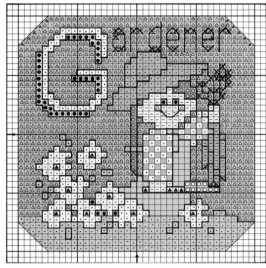

Stitch Count: 40 x 40 (G)

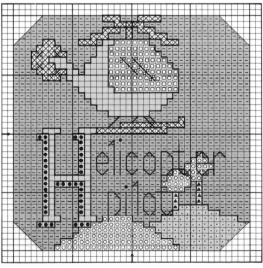

Stitch Count: 40 x 40 (H)

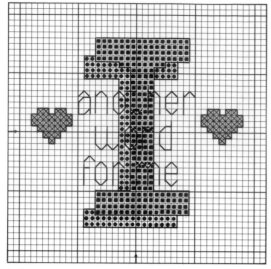

Stitch Count: 36 x 32 (I)

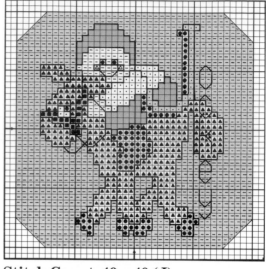

Stitch Count: 40 x 40 (J)

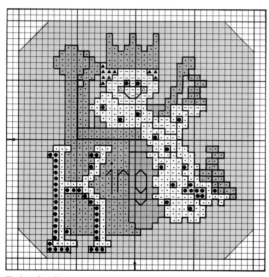

Stitch Count: 40 x 40 (K)

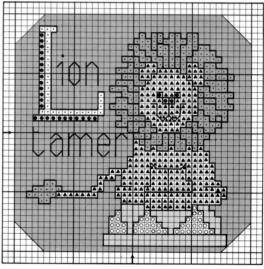

Stitch Count: 40 x 40 (L)

Stitch Count: 40 x 40 (M)

Stitch Count: 40 x 40 (N)

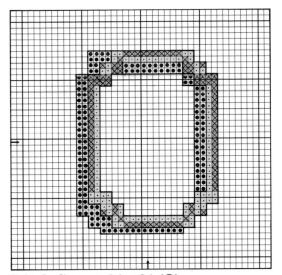

Stitch Count: 24 x 31 (O)

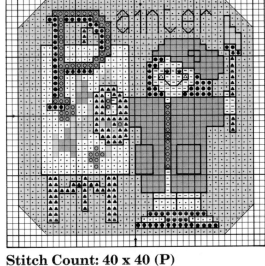

Stitch Count: 40 x 40 (P)

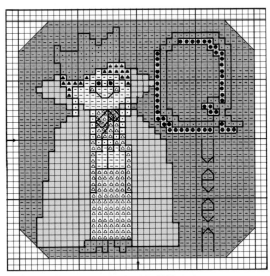

Stitch Count: 40 x 40 (Q)

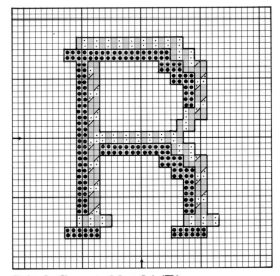

Stitch Count: 26 x 34 (R)

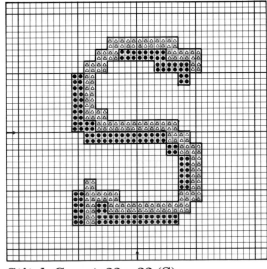

Stitch Count: 22 x 32 (S)

Stitch Count: 40 x 40 (T)

Stitch Count: 40 x 40 (U)

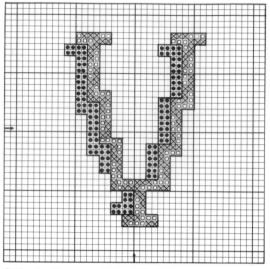

Stitch Count: 24 x 33 (V)

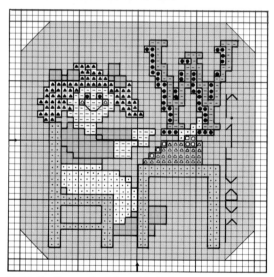

Stitch Count: 40 x 40 (W)

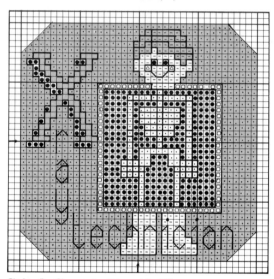

Stitch Count: 40 x 40 (X)

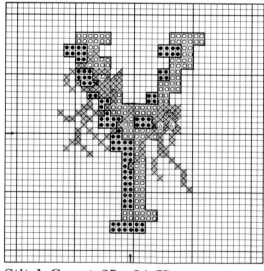

Stitch Count: 25 x 34 (Y)

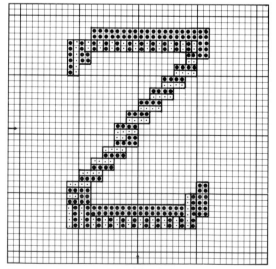

Stitch Count: 24 x 34 (Z)

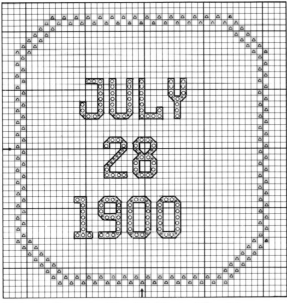

Stitch Count: 43 x 46 (Date Block)

Stitch Count: 43 x 46 (Weight Block)

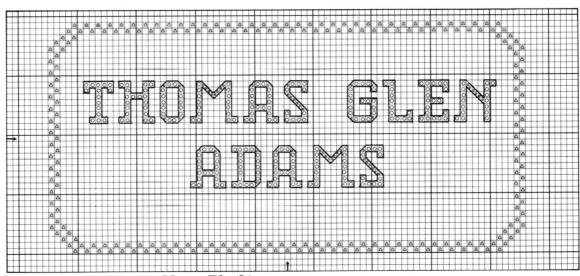

Stitch Count: 81 x 39 (Name Block)

NOVEMBER 17
National Young Reader's Day

Let a book steal your imagination and sweep you up into a world of clouds and dreams. To celebrate the joys of reading, National Young Reader's Day was established in 1989 by the Book It! National Reading Incentive Program and the Center for the Book in the Library of Congress. Schools, libraries, and entire communities nationwide observe this day with activities highlighting the importance of literacy.

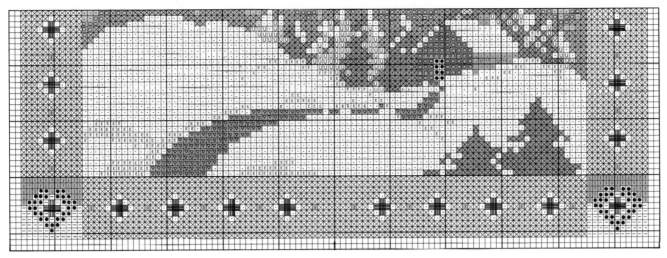

Stitch Count: 112 x 167

The Magic of a Book

SAMPLE

Stitched on ash rose Murano 30 over 2 threads, the finished design size is 7½" x 11⅛". The fabric was cut 14" x 18". Have a professional framer construct a unique mat by covering mat board with quilted fabric.

FABRICS	DESIGN SIZES
Aida 11	10⅛" x 15⅛"
Aida 14	8" x 11⅞"
Aida 18	6¼" x 9¼"
Hardanger 22	5⅛" x 7⅝"

MATERIALS

Completed cross-stitch on ash rose Murano 30
1 (16" x 20") piece of thin pre-quilted fabric

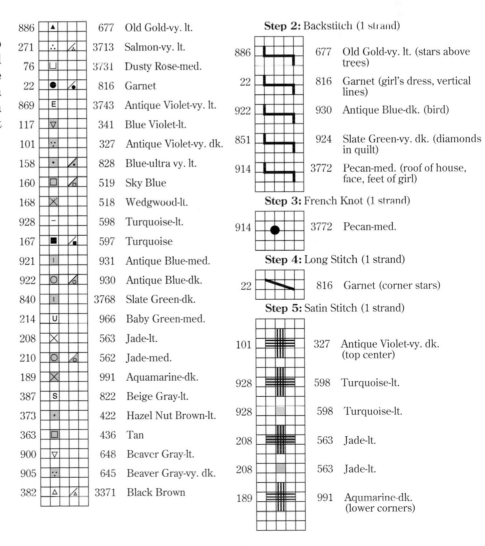

Anchor **DMC (used for sample)**

Step 1: Cross-stitch (2 strands)

Anchor	Symbol	DMC	Color
1	·		White
933	+	3774	Peach Pecan-med.
4146	○	950	Peach Pecan-dk.
886	▲	677	Old Gold-vy. lt.
271	∴	3713	Salmon-vy. lt.
76	⊔	3731	Dusty Rose-med.
22	●	816	Garnet
869	E	3743	Antique Violet-vy. lt.
117	▽	341	Blue Violet-lt.
101	∵	327	Antique Violet-vy. dk.
158	·	828	Blue-ultra vy. lt.
160	□	519	Sky Blue
168	⊠	518	Wedgwood-lt.
928	–	598	Turquoise-lt.
167	■	597	Turquoise
921	I	931	Antique Blue-med.
922	○	930	Antique Blue-dk.
840	I	3768	Slate Green-dk.
214	U	966	Baby Green-med.
208	╳	563	Jade-lt.
210	○	562	Jade-med.
189	╳	991	Aquamarine-dk.
387	S	822	Beige Gray-lt.
373	·	422	Hazel Nut Brown-lt.
363	□	436	Tan
900	▽	648	Beaver Gray-lt.
905	∵	645	Beaver Gray-vy. dk.
382	△	3371	Black Brown

Step 2: Backstitch (1 strand)

Anchor	DMC	Color
886	677	Old Gold-vy. lt. (stars above trees)
22	816	Garnet (girl's dress, vertical lines)
922	930	Antique Blue-dk. (bird)
851	924	Slate Green-vy. dk. (diamonds in quilt)
914	3772	Pecan-med. (roof of house, face, feet of girl)

Step 3: French Knot (1 strand)

Anchor	DMC	Color
914	3772	Pecan-med.

Step 4: Long Stitch (1 strand)

Anchor	DMC	Color
22	816	Garnet (corner stars)

Step 5: Satin Stitch (1 strand)

Anchor	DMC	Color
101	327	Antique Violet-vy. dk. (top center)
928	598	Turquoise-lt.
928	598	Turquoise-lt.
208	563	Jade-lt.
208	563	Jade-lt.
189	991	Aqumarine-dk. (lower corners)

NOVEMBER 25
Thanksgiving

In 1789, during his initial year as president, George Washington declared the first official Thanksgiving Day, although feasts celebrating abundant harvests had been held since the Pilgrims arrived in 1620. Today, the event contains many elements of past Thanksgivings as we celebrate the autumn harvest, religious observances, and national patriotism. This design from artist Trice Boerens draws its images from our rural heritage in celebration of America's bounty.

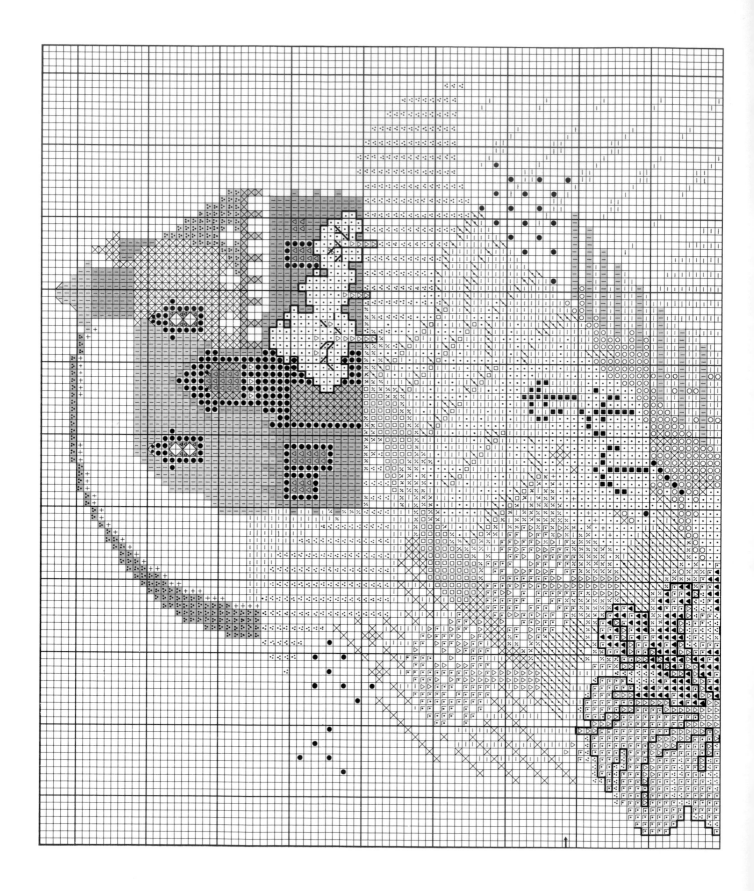

124

Stitch Count: 107 x 143

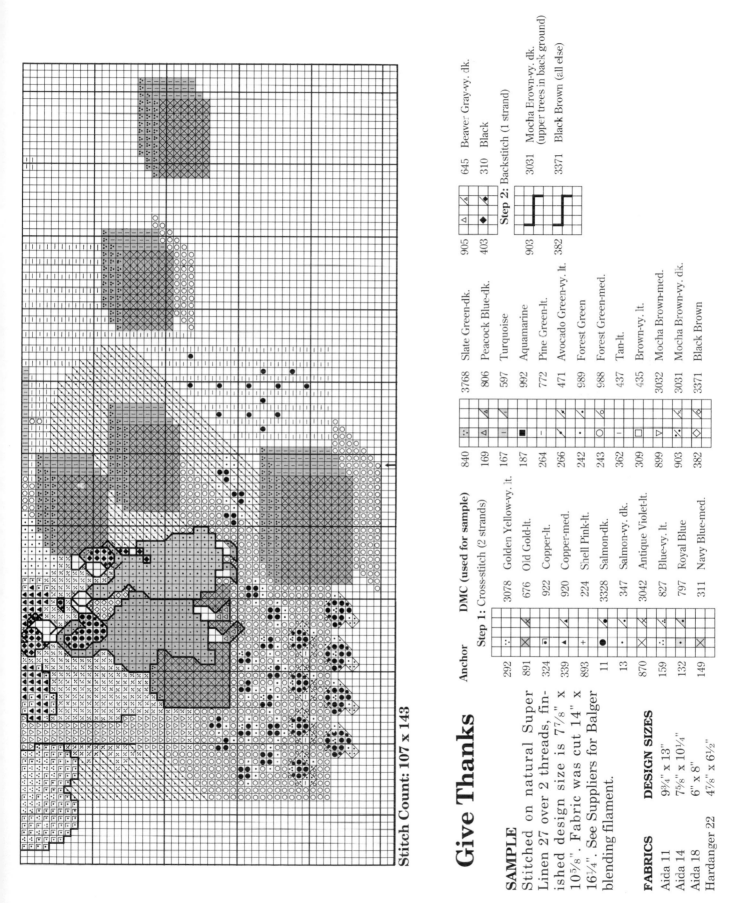

Give Thanks

SAMPLE

Stitched on natural Super Linen 27 over 2 threads, finished design size is 7⅞" x 10⅝". Fabric was cut 14" x 16¼". See Suppliers for Balger blending filament.

FABRICS	DESIGN SIZES
Aida 11	9¾" x 13"
Aida 14	7⅝" x 10¼"
Aida 18	6" x 8"
Hardanger 22	4⅞" x 6½"

Anchor		DMC (used for sample)	
		Step 1: Cross-stitch (2 strands)	
292	∴	3078	Golden Yellow-vy. lt.
891	⊠	676	Old Gold-lt.
324	⊡	922	Copper-lt.
339	▲	920	Copper-med.
893	+	224	Shell Pink-lt.
11	●	3328	Salmon-dk.
13	·	347	Salmon-vy. dk.
870	⊠	3042	Antique Violet-lt.
159	∴	827	Blue-vy. lt.
132	·	797	Royal Blue
149	⊠	311	Navy Blue-med.
840	∴	3768	Slate Green-dk.
169	△	806	Peacock Blue-dk.
167	—	597	Turquoise
187	■	992	Aquamarine
264	-	772	Pine Green-lt.
266	◣	471	Avocado Green-vy. lt.
242	·	989	Forest Green
243	○	988	Forest Green-med.
362	—	437	Tan-lt.
309	□	435	Brown-vy. lt.
899	▽	3032	Mocha Brown-med.
903	⚹	3031	Mocha Brown-vy. dk.
382	◇	3371	Black Brown
905	△	645	Beaver Gray-vy. dk.
403	◆	310	Black
		Step 2: Backstitch (1 strand)	
903		3031	Mocha Brown-vy. dk. (upper trees in back ground)
382		3371	Black Brown (all else)

125

DECEMBER 24
Christmas Eve

*Look closely at
this Christmas stocking
and you will see an
enchanted world of toys,
beribboned gifts, and other
delightful surprises.
A sampling of stitches,
metallic threads, tiny
beads, and richly colored
ribbons give the
design both texture
and sparkle. When the
clock strikes midnight,
you might expect the toys
actually to come to life.*

Toyland Stocking

SAMPLE

Stitched on white Aida 14 over 1 thread, the finished design size is 7⅞" x 14¼". The fabric was cut 14" x 20". See Suppliers for Mill Hill Beads and Balger blending filament.

FABRICS	DESIGN SIZES
Aida 11	10" x 18⅛"
Aida 18	6⅛" x 11⅛"
Hardanger 22	5" x 9⅛"

MATERIALS

Completed cross-stitch on white Aida 14
1 yard of taupe fabric; matching thread
½ yard (45"-wide) flannel
½ yard (⅜"-wide) cream satin ribbon; matching thread
½ yard (1/16"-wide) teal satin ribbon; matching thread

DIRECTIONS

1. For stocking front, cut design piece ½" from side and bottom edges of design and 1½" from top of design. With wrong sides facing and using design piece as pattern, cut 1 piece for front lining from taupe fabric, adding an additional 1¾" to top for cuff. For stocking back and lining, fold remaining taupe fabric in half, with wrong sides facing. Place top edge of design piece on fold and cut 1 back/lining piece through both layers. Do not cut fold. From remaining taupe fabric, cut 1½"-wide bias strips, piecing as needed to equal 40". Set aside. Using design piece as pattern, cut 2 stocking pieces from flannel for interlining.

2. To assemble stocking front, stack taupe front lining piece (right side down); 1 flannel piece; design piece (right side up). Align side and bottom raw edges; baste together. To form cuff, fold 1¾" of taupe fabric at top of front lining piece to front of design piece. Turn straight raw edge of front lining piece under ¼", aligning with top edge of stitched design; slipstitch.

To assemble stocking back, sandwich remaining flannel piece between folded stocking back/lining piece.

3. With lining sides facing and raw edges aligned, stack stocking front on stocking back and baste, leaving top open. To bind edges, with right sides facing and raw edges aligned, stitch bias strip around sides and bottom of stocking, using ⅜" seam. Fold bias strip over raw edge to back, turn under ⅜", and slipstitch to back.

4. To make hanger, fold cream ribbon in half and knot 1½" below fold, leaving long tails. Tack knot to upper right corner of stocking. Fold teal ribbon into a multilooped bow and tack below cream knot.

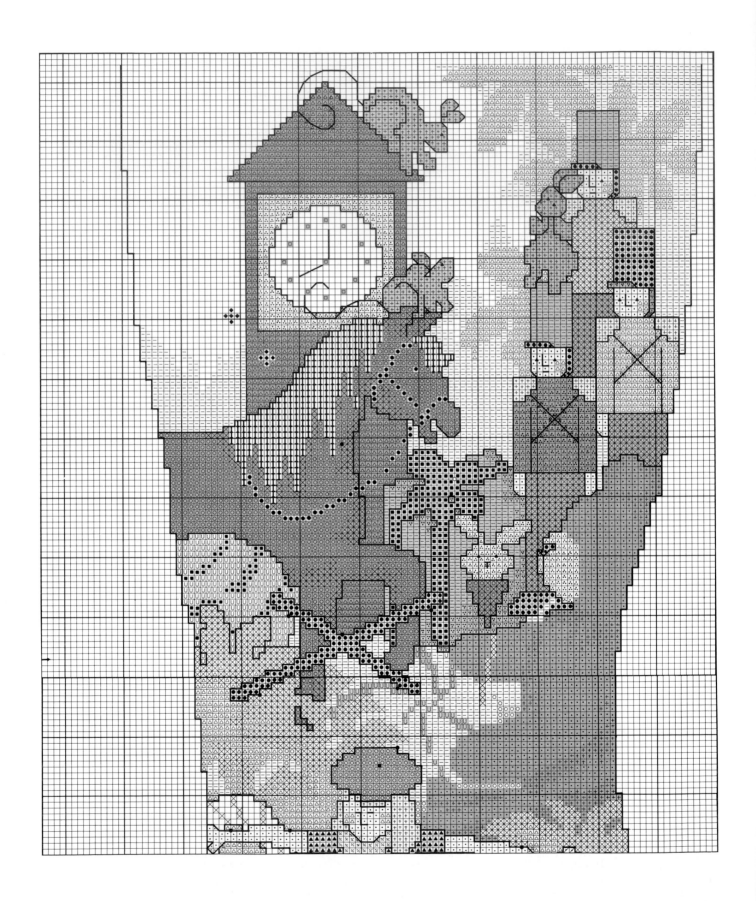

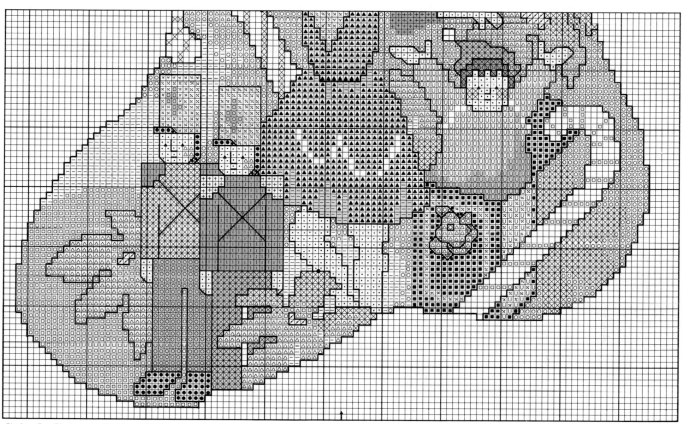

Stitch Count: 110 x 200

Anchor			DMC (used for sample)	
Step 1: Cross-stitch (2 strands)				
292	+	⁄	3078	Golden Yellow-vy. lt.
890	⁄		729	Old Gold-med.
933	·	⁄	3774	Peach Pecan-med.
324	I	⁄	922	Copper-lt.
892	∴	⁄	225	Shell Pink-vy. lt.
892	□		225	Shell Pink-vy. lt. (1 strand)
9	△	⁄	760	Salmon
13	✕		347	Salmon-vy. dk.
969	∴		316	Antique Mauve-med.
104	U		210	Lavender-med.
101	■	◢	327	Antique Violet-vy. dk.
118	U		340	Blue Violet-med.
121	◯	⁄	794	Cornflower Blue-lt.
131	▲		798 051HL	Delft-dk. (2 strands)+ Sapphire Balger blending filament (1 strand)
922	✕	⁄	930	Antique Blue-dk.
928	−	⁄	598	Turquoise-lt.
167	∴	⁄	597	Turquoise
266	−	⁄	3347	Yellow Green-med. (1 strand)

246	◯	⁄	986	Forest Green-vy. dk.
393	+	⁄	3790	Beige Gray-ultra vy. dk.
309	◯	⁄	435	Brown-vy. lt.
371	✕		433	Brown-med.
397	△		3072	Beaver Gray-vy. lt.
399	⁒	⁄	452	Shell Gray-med.
403	●	⁄	310	Black

Step 2: Backstitch (1 strand)

309		435	Brown-vy. lt. (horse's mane)
236		3799	Pewter Gray-vy. dk. (all else)

Step 3: French Knot (1 strand)

236	▲		3799	Pewter Gray-vy. dk.

Step 4: Beadwork (Mill Hill Beads)

◆		00968	Red
□		00020	Royal Blue
▩		00330	Copper

Step 5: Turkish Tufting Stitch (For each stitch, backstitch over 1 thread; working over the backstitch, make a loop stitch about 1/8" deep. Continue stitching to fill area, then clip all loops.)

899	·		3782	Mocha Brown-lt.
393	+	⁄	3790	Beige Gray-ultra vy. dk.

Step 6: Couching

✝		013	Beige Balger braid #16 (1 strand) couched with DMC floss 3774 Peach Pecan-med. (2 strands)
✕		FR21	Frizz (1 strand) couched with DMC floss (1 strand) 598 Turquoise-lt.

Step 7: Attach marionette strings.

●			Royal Blue 1/16" ribbon braid

Step 8: Attach bow. Cut 1 (8") 4-strand piece of each floss. Make 1/2"-deep loops to form a bow. Tack centers to design piece.

104	⊕		210	Lavender-med.
118	⊕		340	Blue Violet-med.

Step 9: Attach ribbon. Tie 4" piece of ribbon in knot; tack.

■		1/8" red ribbon

DECEMBER 25
Christmas Day

Christmas is a magical time when friends and family come together, sharing love, laughter, and special gifts. Perhaps the dearest gifts that remind others of your love are those made by hand. In this section, you'll find exciting designs for gift giving: three-dimensional Santas with fluffy, snowy-white beards and Julnisse, the Danish spirit of Christmas.

Santa Trio

SAMPLE

Stitched on Needlepoint Canvas 14 over 1 thread, the finished design size is 4⅞" x 7⅛" for Santa with Holly, 3⅝" x 6¾" for Santa with Toys, and 4⅛" x 6⅞" for Santa with Bag. The canvas was cut 11" x 14" for Santa with Holly, 10" x 13" for Santa with Toys, and 11" x 13" for Santa with Bag. See Suppliers for special thread.

MATERIALS for Santa with Holly

Completed cross-stitch on Needlepoint Canvas 14
10 red seed beads
3 (⅜") green tear-shaped beads
White filament-fiber curly hair

DIRECTIONS

1. For beard, tack various lengths of curly hair to beard area (see graph).

2. Tack beads to canvas at right side of head as desired to resemble holly and berries (see photo).

MATERIALS for Santa with Toys

Completed cross-stitch on Needlepoint Canvas 14
Gold metallic thread
5 or 6 miniature ornaments
1 (2½"-long) chenille Christmas tree
White filament-fiber curly hair
Hot-glue gun and glue sticks

DIRECTIONS

1. Cut a 6" piece of gold thread for each ornament. Tie 1 length of thread around each ornament and tack to left side of belt (see photo).

2. Glue tree at an angle to Santa's shoulder, next to beard (see photo).

3. For beard and hair, see Step 1 of Santa with Holly.

MATERIALS for Santa with Bag

Completed cross-stitch on Needlepoint Canvas 14
1 (2" x 3") piece of gold satin; matching thread
Gold metallic thread
Small amount of stuffing
White filament-fiber curly hair

DIRECTIONS

1. To make bag, fold satin in half to measure 1½" x 2". Using matching thread, stitch ¼" seam along side and bottom edges, rounding corners as shown in Diagram and leaving top open. Trim and clip curves; turn. Turn top raw edge of bag ¼" to inside and hem with a running stitch, using gold metallic thread. Stuff bag. Pull thread to gather and tie thread in a bow on right side of bag. Slipstitch bag to canvas at Santa's right hand (see photo).

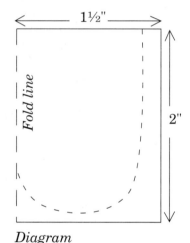

Diagram

2. For beard, see Step 1 of Santa with Holly.

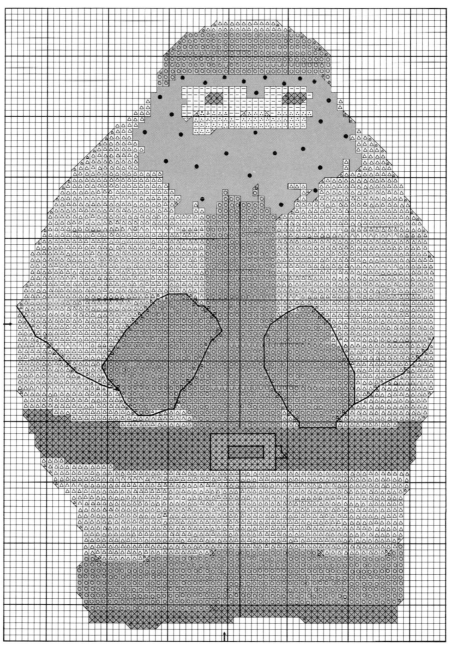

Stitch Count: 69 x 100 (Santa with Holly)

Paternayan Persian Yarn and Pearl Cotton (used for sample)

Step 1: Cross-stitch (2 strands)

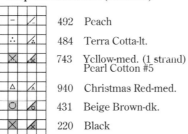

- /		492	Peach
∴ ◢		484	Terra Cotta-lt.
⊠ ◣		743	Yellow-med. (1 strand) Pearl Cotton #5
△ ◿		940	Christmas Red-med.
○ ◖		431	Beige Brown-dk.
⊠ ◣		220	Black

Step 2: Backstitch (1 strand)

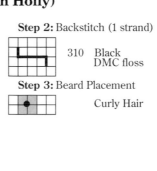

310 Black
DMC floss

Step 3: Beard Placement

Curly Hair

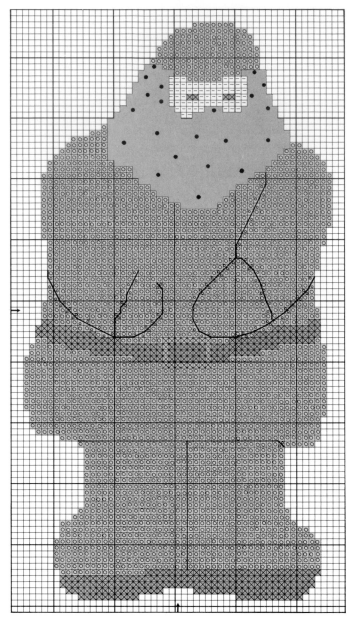

Stitch Count: 51 x 95 (Santa with Toys)

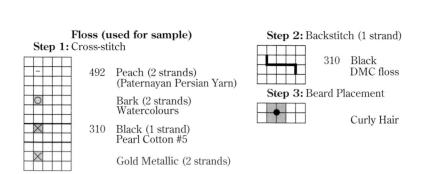

Floss (used for sample)

Step 1: Cross-stitch

−
◯
✕
✕

492   Peach (2 strands)
        (Paternayan Persian Yarn)

        Bark (2 strands)
        Watercolours

310   Black (1 strand)
        Pearl Cotton #5

        Gold Metallic (2 strands)

Step 2: Backstitch (1 strand)

310   Black
        DMC floss

Step 3: Beard Placement

        Curly Hair

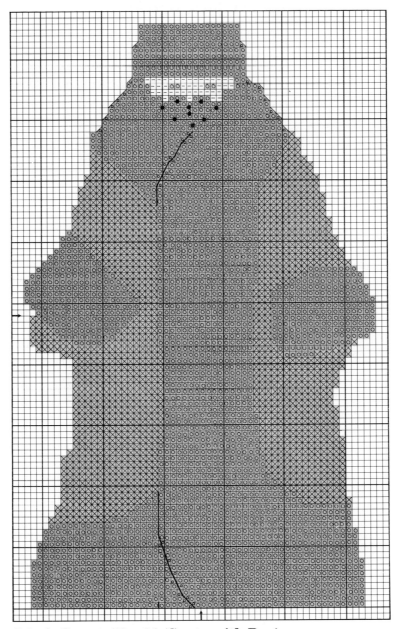

Stitch Count: 58 x 96 (Santa with Bag)

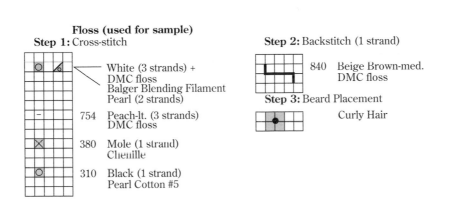

Floss (used for sample)

Step 1: Cross-stitch

○	╱ White (3 strands) + DMC floss Balger Blending Filament Pearl (2 strands)
−	754 Peach-lt. (3 strands) DMC floss
✕	380 Mole (1 strand) Chenille
○	310 Black (1 strand) Pearl Cotton #5

Step 2: Backstitch (1 strand)

840 Beige Brown-med. DMC floss

Step 3: Beard Placement

Curly Hair

Julnisse

SAMPLE
Stitched on pewter Murano 30 over 2 threads, the finished design size is 8¾" x 11½". The fabric was cut 15" x 18".

FABRICS	DESIGN SIZES
Aida 11	11⅞" x 15¾"
Aida 14	9⅜" x 12⅜"
Aida 18	7¼" x 9⅝"
Hardanger 22	6" x 7⅞"

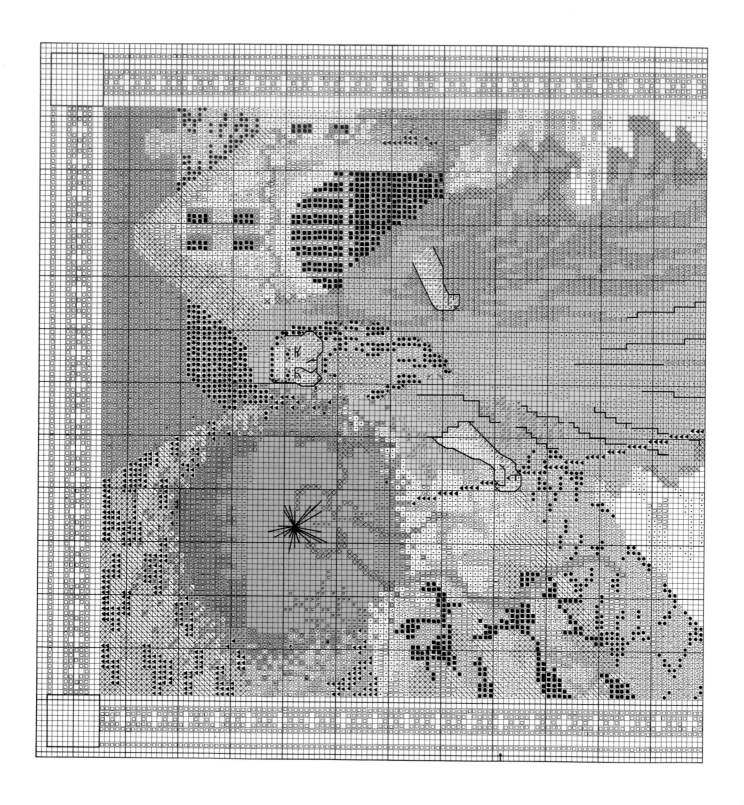

140

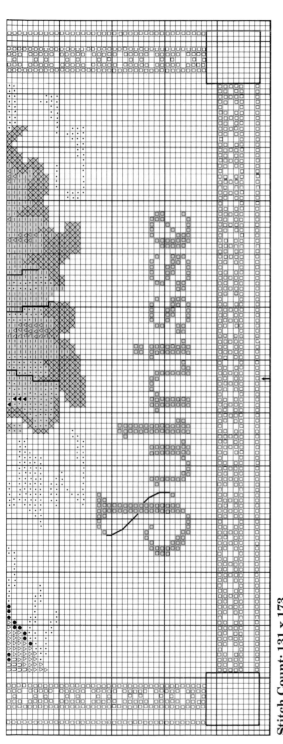

Stitch Count: 131 x 173

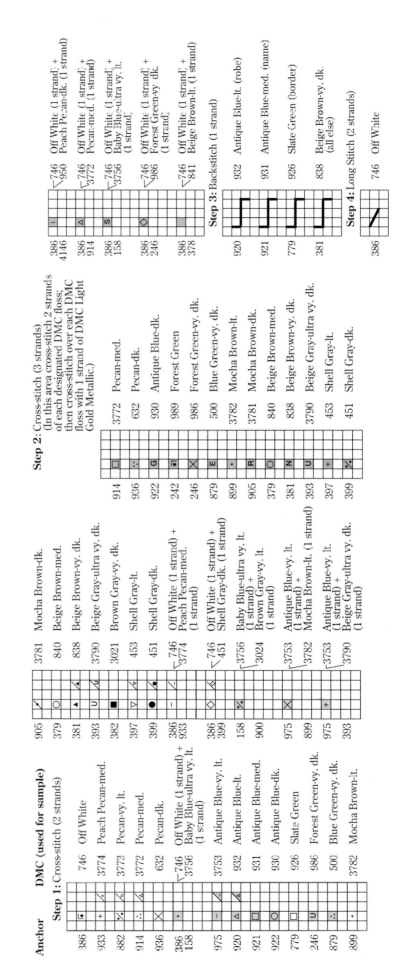

Anchor		DMC (used for sample)

Step 1: Cross-stitch (2 strands)

386	●	746	Off White
933	+	3774	Peach Pecan-med.
882	▨	3773	Pecan-vy. lt.
914	▨	3772	Pecan-med.
936	✕	632	Pecan-dk.
386 158	•	746 3756	Off White (1 strand) + Baby Blue-ultra vy. lt. (1 strand)
975	−	3753	Antique Blue-vy. lt.
920	△	932	Antique Blue-lt.
921	□	931	Antique Blue-med.
922	○	930	Antique Blue-dk.
779	□	926	Slate Green
246	U	986	Forest Green-vy. dk.
879	∴	500	Blue Green-vy. dk.
899	•	3782	Mocha Brown-lt.
905	◿	3781	Mocha Brown-dk.
379	○	840	Beige Brown-med.
381	◣	838	Beige Brown-vy. dk.
393	U	3790	Beige Gray-ultra vy. dk.
382	■	3021	Brown Gray-vy. dk.
397	▽	453	Shell Gray-lt.
399	●	451	Shell Gray-dk.
386 933	−	746 3774	Off White (1 strand) + Peach Pecan-med. (1 strand)
386 399	◇	746 451	Off White (1 strand) + Shell Gray-dk. (1 strand)
158	✕	3756	Baby Blue-ultra vy. lt. (1 strand) +
900		3024	Brown Gray-vy. lt. (1 strand)
975	✕	3753	Antique Blue-vy. lt. (1 strand) +
899		3782	Mocha Brown-lt. (1 strand)
975	+	3753	Antique Blue-vy. lt. (1 strand) +
393		3790	Beige Gray-ultra vy. dk. (1 strand)

Step 2: Cross-stitch (3 strands)
(In this area cross-stitch 2 strands of each designated DMC floss; then cross-stitch over each DMC floss with 1 strand of DMC Light Gold Metallic.)

914	□	3772	Pecan-med.
936	∷	632	Pecan-dk.
922	G	930	Antique Blue-dk.
242	◩	989	Forest Green
246	✕	986	Forest Green-vy. dk.
879	E	500	Blue Green-vy. dk.
899	•	3782	Mocha Brown-lt.
905	R	3781	Mocha Brown-dk.
379	○	840	Beige Brown-med.
381	N	838	Beige Brown-vy. dk.
393	U	3790	Beige Gray-ultra vy. dk.
397	+	453	Shell Gray-lt.
399	✕	451	Shell Gray-dk.
386 4146	I	746 950	Off White (1 strand) + Peach Pecan-dk. (1 strand)
386 914	◁	746 3772	Off White (1 strand) + Pecan-med. (1 strand)
386 158	S	746 3756	Off White (1 strand) + Baby Blue-ultra vy. lt. (1 strand)
386 246	◇	746 986	Off White (1 strand) + Forest Green-vy. dk. (1 strand)
386 378		746 841	Off White (1 strand) + Beige Brown-lt. (1 strand)

Step 3: Backstitch (1 strand)

920		932	Antique Blue-lt. (robe)
921		931	Antique Blue-med. (name)
779		926	Slate Green (border)
381		838	Beige Brown-vy. dk. (all else)

Step 4: Long Stitch (2 strands)

| 386 | | 746 | Off White |

General Instructions

CROSS-STITCH

Fabrics: Most designs in this book are worked on even-weave fabrics made especially for cross-stitch and can be found in your local needlework shop. If you cannot find a particular fabric, see Suppliers for ordering information. Fabrics used for models are identified in sample information by color, name, and thread count per inch.

Preparing Fabric: Cut fabric at least 3" larger on all sides than finished design size, or cut as indicated in sample information, to ensure enough space for matting, framing, and other finishing techniques for stitched piece. To keep fabric from fraying, whipstitch or machine-zigzag along raw edges or apply liquid ravel preventer.

Needles: Choose a needle that will slip easily through fabric holes without piercing fabric threads. For fabric with 11 or fewer threads per inch, use needle size 24; for 14 threads per inch, use needle size 24 or 26; for 18 or more threads per inch, use needle size 26. Never leave needle in design area of fabric. It may leave rust or a permanent impression on fabric.

Hoop or Frame: Using a hoop or frame keeps fabric taut and makes it easier to make uniform stitches. Select a hoop or stretcher bar frame large enough to hold entire design. Place screw or clamp of hoop in a 10 o'clock position (or 2 o'clock, if you are left-handed) to keep it from catching floss.

Centering Design: To find center of *fabric*, fold it in half from top to bottom and then from left to right. The intersection of folds is center. To find center of *graph*, follow vertical and horizontal arrows until they intersect. Begin stitching center of design at center of fabric.

Finished Design Size: To determine size of finished design, divide stitch count by number of threads per inch of fabric. When design is stitched over 2 threads, divide stitch count by half the threads per inch.

Floss: Use 18" lengths of floss. For best coverage, separate strands. Dampen with wet sponge. Then put back together number of strands called for in color code.

Securing Floss: Bring needle and most of floss up through fabric, leaving a 1" tail of floss on underside. Secure floss tail with first few stitches.

Another method for securing floss is the waste knot. Knot floss and bring needle down through fabric about 1" from where first stitch will be taken. Plan placement of knot so that first 4 or 5 stitches cover and secure 1" of floss on back of fabric. After floss is secured, cut off knot.

To secure floss after stitching is completed, run needle under 4 or 5 stitches on back of design and clip ends close to fabric.

Stitching Method: For smooth stitches, use the push-and-pull method. Starting on wrong side of fabric, bring needle straight up, pulling floss completely through to right side. Reinsert needle and bring it back straight down, pulling needle and floss completely through to back of fabric. Keep floss flat but do not pull thread tight. For even stitches, tension should be consistent throughout.

Carrying Floss: To carry floss, weave it under previously worked stitches on back. Do not carry floss across any fabric that is not or will not be stitched. Loose strands, especially dark ones, will show through fabric.

Twisted Floss: Floss covers best when lying flat. If floss begins to twist, suspend needle and allow floss to unwind itself.

Cleaning Completed Work: When stitching is complete, soak finished piece in cold water with mild soap for 5 to 10 minutes. Rinse thoroughly. Roll work in towel to remove excess water; do not wring. Place work face down on dry towel and press with warm iron until work is dry.

BEADWORK

First, attach bead to fabric with diagonal stitch, from lower left to upper right. Secure bead by returning floss through bead, from lower right to upper left (Diagram A). When working in rows, complete a row of diagonal half-cross stitches before returning to secure all beads.

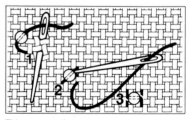

Diagram A

WASTE CANVAS

Cut waste canvas 1" larger on all sides than finished design. Baste waste canvas to fabric to be stitched. Each stitch is over 1 unit (2 threads). When stitching is complete, use a spray bottle to dampen stitched area with cold water. Pull waste canvas threads out 1 at a time with tweezers. It is easier to pull all threads running in 1 direction first; then pull out opposite threads. Allow stitching to dry; then place face down on a towel and iron.

COMMON STITCHES

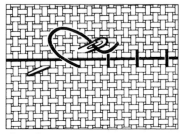

Couching

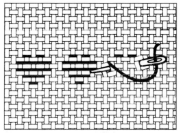

Satin Stitch

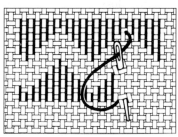

Long Stitch

Three-quarter Stitch: Three-quarter stitch is indicated on graph when a symbol fills only half of a square (Diagram D). If you are working over 1 thread, the short understitch will pierce the fabric thread; if you are working over 2 threads, it will slip through the hole between the 2 threads. In each case the long stitch is the overstitch, even though in some cases this may violate the rule that all stitches should be worked from left to right and back again.

When 2 symbols occupy a single square on the graph, make a three-quarter stitch and a quarter stitch to fill the square. Which symbol applies to which stitch depends on the line you want to emphasize. Use three-quarter stitch to express dominant line or color (Diagram E).

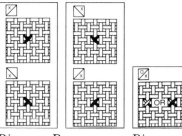

Diagram D   *Diagram E*

Backstitch: Complete all cross-stitches before working backstitches or other accent stitches. Working from right to left with 1 strand of floss (unless indicated otherwise in color code), bring needle up at A, down at B, and up at C. Going back down at A, continue in this manner (Diagram G).

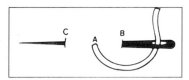

Diagram G

SEWING HINT

Bias Strips: Bias strips are used to make ruffles, binding, or corded piping. To cut bias strips, fold fabric at a 45° angle to grain of fabric and crease. Cut on crease. Cut strips the width indicated in directions, cutting parallel to first cutting line. Ends of bias strips should be cut on grain of fabric. Place right sides of ends together as shown and stitch with ¼" seam (Diagram H). Continue to piece strips until they are length indicated in directions.

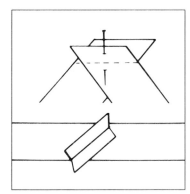

Diagram H

Cross-stitch: Make 1 cross-stitch for each symbol on chart. Bring needle up at A, down at B, up at C, and down again at D (Diagram B). For rows, stitch across fabric from left to right to make half-crosses and then back to complete stitch (Diagram C). All bottom half-crosses should slant in the same direction; top half-crosses should slant in the opposite direction.

Diagram B

Diagram C

French Knot: Bring needle up at A. Wrap floss around needle twice (unless indicated otherwise in directions). Insert needle beside A, pulling floss until it fits snugly around needle. Pull needle through to back (Diagram F).

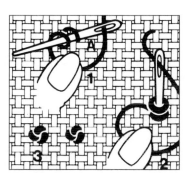

Diagram F

143

Suppliers

All products are available retail from Shepherd's Bush, 220 24th Street, Ogden, UT 84401; (801) 399-4546; or for a merchant near you, write the following suppliers:

Zweigart Fabrics—
Zweigart/Joan Toggitt Ltd., Weston Canal Plaza, 2 Riverview Drive, Somerset, NJ 08873

Zweigart Fabrics used:
White Aida 14
Cream Aida 14
Ash Rose Aida 14
Linaida 14
Rustico 14
Needlepoint Canvas 14
Waste Canvas 14
Cream Cork Linen 19
Sand Dublin Linen 25
White Linda 27
Apricot Pastel Linen 28
Carnation Pastel Linen 28
Daffodil Pastel Linen 28
Periwinkle Pastel Linen 28
Pistachio Pastel Linen 28
Ash Rose Murano 30
Cracked Wheat Murano 30
Pewter Murano 30

White Belfast Linen 32
Cream Belfast Linen 32
Raw Belfast Linen 32

Vanessa-Ann Damask 28, Vanessa-Ann Afghan Weave 18, Abigail Porcelain Doll Parts— Chapelle Designers, P.O. Box 9252, Newgate Station, Ogden, UT 84409

Cream Jobelan 28 and Natural Linen 28—Wichelt Imports, Inc., Rural Route 1, Stoddard, WI 54658

Natural Super Linen 27 and Rich Cranberry Royal Classic 14—Charles Craft, P.O. Box 1049, Laurinburg, NC 28352

Filatura Di Crosa Sympathie #934—Stacy Charles Collection, 119 Green Street, Brooklyn, NY 11222

Paternayan Persian Yarn— Johnson Creative Arts, Inc., P.O. Box 158, 445 Main Street, Townsend, MA 01474

Overture Yarn—Rainbow Gallery, 7412 Fulton Avenue, Unit 5, North Hollywood, CA 91605

Balger Products, Gold Metallic Thread—Kreinik Mfg. Co., Inc., P.O. Box 1966, Parkersburg, WV 26102

Watercolours—The Caron Collection, 67 Poland Street, Bridgeport, CT 06605

Satin Ribbons—C.M. Offray and Son, Inc., 41 Madison Avenue, New York, NY 10010

Mill Hill Beads—Gay Bowles Sales, 1310 Plainfield Avenue, Janesville, WI 53547

Acrylic Paints—Delta Technical Coatings, Inc., 2550 Pellissier Place, Whittier, CA 90601

Stuffing—Fairfield Processing Corp., P.O. Drawer 1157, 88 Rose Hill Avenue, Danbury, CT 06813-1157

Glue—Aleene's, 85 Industrial Way, Buellton, CA 93427

Sewing Machine—Bernina of America

Jacket Motif

SAMPLE
Stitched on rich cranberry Royal Classic 14 over 1 thread. To create border shown on back cover, complete 1 corner motif and 3½ border repeats for width measurement; complete 1 corner motif and 5 border repeats for length measurement. Rotate graph clockwise a ¼ turn at each corner to complete.

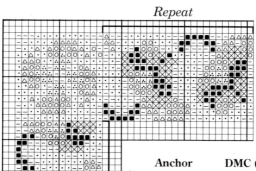

Repeat

Anchor		DMC (used for sample)	
		Step 1: Cross-stitch (2 strands)	
303	·	742	Tangerine-lt.
47	O	321	Christmas Red
20	X	498	Christmas Red-dk.
98	∴	553	Violet-med.
119	−	333	Blue Violet-dk.
168	△	807	Peacock Blue
189	■	991	Aquamarine-dk.